Saint Joan

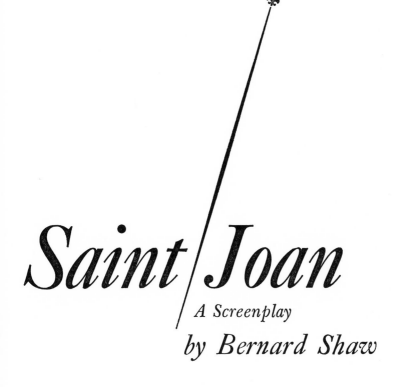

Saint/Joan

A Screenplay
by Bernard Shaw

edited and with an Introduction by
Bernard F. Dukore

University of Washington Press / Seattle and London

To Joyce

Contents

Illustrations

Introduction

Bernard Shaw's first play to reach the screen was the same play whose later adaptation as a film is the substance of this book, *Saint Joan*. In the summer of 1927, Widgery Newman directed the Cathedral scene from *Joan* for Phonofilms (the DeForest Phonofilm Company, a motion picture firm which synchronized records with silent films), with Sybil Thorndike, who created the role in England in 1924, as Joan.[1] This film-and-record experiment, one of several early efforts to make the screen talk, appeared on the eve of talking movies: in October, 1927, *The Jazz Singer*, the first "talkie," opened.

Before the advent of sound, Shaw refused to allow moviemakers to film his plays. "A play with the words left out," he maintained, "is a play spoiled." Silent movie versions of plays with dialogue are good only when the dialogue is so bad that its omission is an advantage. "Of course," Shaw realized, "that is a very large exception in point of bulk; but the moment you come to classic drama the omission of the words and the presentation of the mere scenario is very much as if you offered the wire

---

[1] Raymond Mander and Joe Mitchenson, *Theatrical Companion to Shaw* (London: Rockliff, 1954), p. 321. See Appendix A for a list of films written by Shaw. A Czech adaptation of Shaw's novel *Cashel Byron's Profession* was made in 1921 under the title *Roman Boxera*. See Donald P. Costello, *The Serpent's Eye: Shaw and the Cinema* (Notre Dame, Ind.: University of Notre Dame Press, 1965), p. 153. I am greatly indebted to Professor Costello's extremely valuable book, and throughout this introduction I make extensive use of the factual material he records. His conclusions, however, generally differ from my own. According to Costello, Shaw was a good screenwriter only when his practice departed from his theory and a bad screenwriter when Shavian theory and practice coincided (as it did, according to him, in *Major Barbara*). Costello's viewpoint is well articulated, and I am glad to direct readers interested in examining our differences to *The Serpent's Eye*, especially pp. 109–12 and p. 146.

skeleton which supports a sculptor's modelling clay as a statue." [2] He regarded his own plays as classic drama. "I am a Classic," he proclaimed in 1920. "I have never pretended to be anything else." [3]

With the advent of sound, Shaw reconsidered his refusals, for now the motion pictures could accommodate the classic drama. Only motion picture makers stood in the way. "Of course the talkies have come to stay," Shaw told an interviewer in 1929. "Will you then allow your plays to be made into talking pictures?" asked the interviewer. "Not until I am satisfied that there is a producer who . . . knows his job," replied Shaw.[4]

"Knowing his job" meant agreeing with Shaw, whose theories of cinema are contrary to those held by film theorists and practitioners. The major issue is whether motion pictures are different from the stage in degree or in kind. Shaw maintained the former, film theorists and film makers the latter. "I see no reason," he said in his 1929 interview, "why *The Apple Cart,* for instance, should not be produced exactly as it stands." While he recognized that different techniques are required, he believed that the art of spoken drama on stage is not *essentially* different from the art of spoken drama on screen. According to the traditional view of cinema, the function of dialogue is minimal: the sparser the better. Once necessary information has been conveyed, dialogue can stop, for it has fulfilled its function. The camera, not language, is primary.

Shaw's point of view was heretical: the photographer should not get out of hand or gain the upper hand, film techniques should not interfere with or interrupt the spoken language, motion picture makers should present drama rather than a display of photography. As he told Lawrence Langner in 1935, the Hollywood "notion of a scenario [is] a man lecturing on a series

[2] Bernard Shaw and Archibald Henderson, "The Drama, the Theatre, and the Films," *Fortnightly Review,* n.s. CXVI (September 1, 1924), 294.

[3] Letter in the *Arts Gazette,* January 31, 1920. In *Shaw on Theatre,* ed. E. J. West (New York: Hill and Wang, 1958), p. 132.

[4] G. W. Bishop, "The Living Talkies: An Interview with Bernard Shaw," *Theatre Guild Magazine,* VII (November, 1929), 32.

of pictures, like the old dioramas of my youth." The picture makers expend miles of film showing people who "expend tons of energy jumping in and out of automobiles, knocking at doors, running up and downstairs, opening and shutting bedroom doors, drawing automatics, being arrested and tried for inexplicable crimes, with intervals of passionate killing" in their "pitiable" efforts to tell a story.

> Scenically, histrionically, photographically, and wastefully, Hollywood is the wonder of the world; but it has no dramatic technique and no literary taste: it will stick a patch of slovenly speakeasy California dialect upon a fine passage of English prose without seeing any difference, like a color-blind man sticking a patch of Highland tartan on his dress trousers. When it gets a good bit of stuff it takes infinite pains to drag it down to its own level, firmly believing, of course, that it is improving it all the time.[5]

That level is a plane of mediocrity. In his discussion of the silent screen, Shaw explained that the film industry's "colossal proportions make mediocrity compulsory." Since movies go round the globe, the film makers do not try to please the intellectuals but instead "aim at the average of an American millionaire and a Chinese coolie, a cathedral town governess and a mining village barmaid. . . ." [6] Shaw did not alter his views when sound was added, for the film industry did not alter its practices.

Still, Hollywood moviemakers wanted to film Shaw's plays. Negotiations usually stopped when Shaw insisted on approval of the final script. In 1933, RKO was considering a film version of *The Devil's Disciple* with John Barrymore as Dick Dudgeon. Shaw not only demanded approval of the script, but explicitly stipulated in advance that Dick's relationship with Judith not be made romantic, for even the slightest suggestion of an amatory motive for his self-sacrifice "would belittle him unbearably and reduce the whole affair to third-rate Hollywood sobstuff." [7] Negotiations ended.

[5] Shaw to Langner, February 15, 1935, in Lawrence Langner, *G.B.S. and the Lunatic* (New York: Atheneum, 1963), p. 225.

[6] Shaw and Henderson, "Drama, Theatre, and Films," p. 290.

[7] Quoted in Costello, *Serpent's Eye*, p. 28.

In the early thirties, British International Pictures made two films of Shaw's plays: *How He Lied to Her Husband* (1931) and *Arms and the Man* (1932). Shaw demanded and secured approval of the final scripts. Since he also supervised the actual filming, he successfully averted attempts at cinematic doctoring. Donald P. Costello relates one such attempt:

> When Frank Launder, a writer for British International, tried to add a little cinematic touch to the film of *How He Lied,* he discovered that Shaw meant what the contract said. Launder thought up a scene where the young lover, in his eagerness to meet his lady, dashes into the apartment and places his opera hat on the head of a piece of sculpture. He suggested that the camera show in a close-up that the piece of sculpture is a bust of Shaw himself. Shaw was not amused; and British International stuck to the contract, and to the script.[8]

The "little cinematic touch," Launder failed to recognize, was inappropriate, for the Philistine Teddy Bompas (Her Husband) would scarcely have a bust of Bernard Shaw in his house; Bompas had, in fact, fallen asleep during a performance of *Candida.*[9] Shaw did not object unwaveringly to references to himself in his works. In the third act of *The Doctor's Dilemma,* Dubedat proclaims himself a disciple of Bernard Shaw, calling him "the most advanced man alive." [10] The amoral artist, however, is a different character from the wealthy Husband. The values and attitudes that Dubedat shuns are among the foundations of Bompas' life; those which Dubedat embraces, Bompas shuns.

[8] *Ibid.,* pp. 33–34.

[9] The specific reference to *Candida* is in the early editions of the play, e.g., *John Bull's Other Island and Major Barbara* (New York: Brentano's, 1908), p. 140. When Shaw revised the play for the Standard Edition—*John Bull's Other Island with How He Lied to Her Husband and Major Barbara* (London: Constable, 1931)—which he used for the film as well as for later reprints of the play, he deleted all references to *Candida.* These deletions, however, do not alter the nature of the characters. For a comparison of the two versions, see my "Shaw Improves Shaw," *Modern Drama,* VI (May, 1963), 26–31. Further references to *How He Lied to Her Husband* and *Major Barbara* are to this edition.

[10] *The Doctor's Dilemma, Getting Married, The Shewing-up of Blanco Posnet* (London: Constable, 1947), pp. 141–42.

In the souvenir program of the 1931 Malvern Festival,[11] where *How He Lied to Her Husband* was shown, Shaw boasted that this film was not merely a silent movie with spoken subtitles. Unlike other talkies,

> the dialogue is continuous from end to end, except where Mr. [Edmund] Gwenn purposely makes a silence more dramatic than words could be, and . . . the entire action takes place in the same room, the usual changes from New York to the Rocky Mountains, from Marseilles to the Sahara, from Mayfair to Monte Carlo, are replaced by changes from the piano to the sideboard, from the window to the door, from the hearth rug to the carpet.[12]

In contrast to the type of movie of which Shaw complained to Lawrence Langner, this film does not have the husband arriving in a taxi, opening the door, climbing the stairs, or any other "baby padding." Shaw does *not* boast that a stationary camera rolls on while a play is being performed, but that *drastic* changes of background are unnecessary for variety. Intercontinental changes of locale "are replaced by" camera changes within the same room.

Shaw did not issue blanket objections to changes of locale or to the addition of scenes. He objected only when they were irrelevant or unnecessary. In the souvenir program of the 1932 Malvern Festival, where the screen version of *Arms and the Man* was shown, he boasts that the medium of film explodes the stage's physical limitations.

> In the play the incident in the battle of Slivnitza, on which the story turns, is not seen: it has to be described in a lady's bedroom. The whole action of the play has to be confined to three scenes, two of them indoors. In the picture the battle is shewn, and the flight of the fugitive whom the heroine shelters. There is no pinning of the characters to one spot: they pass in and out of doors, upstairs and downstairs, into gardens and across mountain country, with a

[11] In 1929, Sir Barry Jackson, founder of the Birmingham Repertory Company, established the Malvern Festival chiefly for the purpose of presenting Shaw's plays. What Bayreuth was to Wagner, he hoped Malvern would be to Shaw.

[12] *Shaw on Theatre*, pp. 205–6.

freedom and variety impossible in the room with three walls which, however scene-painters may disguise it, is always the same old stage.[13]

In the same manner, Shaw tried to transcend the stage's physical limitations in a projected film version of *The Devil's Disciple,* for which he wrote additional scenes extending the action to Philadelphia and England.[14] The new scenes derive from suggestions in the play, setting the mood and substituting for exposition. The opening sequences vividly display a cinematic flair:

1. *Title.*
    On Art Backing of original Congress House:—
    July 4th 1776
THE DECLARATION OF
AMERICAN INDEPENDENCE
    Dissolve to:
2. *Close shot, Thomas Jefferson.* Silent scene.
    Indoors signing the declaration. Silent and businesslike.
2A. Close-up of his signature, and then of the heading D of I engrossed.
3. *Medium shot, flag pole.*
    British Royal Standard flying. It comes down and is replaced by the American flag, revealing the thirteen stars and thirteen stripes of the first Federation.
    Dissolve to:
[4.] *Exterior St. James's Palace. Day.*
    Superimpose *title:*
    The King's Palace, London 1777.

This dissolves to the interior of the royal apartment, where Lord North is trying to explain to King George III the troubles in North America. When North refers to "the New England States," the King interrupts. " 'States!' " he exclaims. "What do you mean

[13] *Ibid.,* pp. 212–13.

[14] Bernard Shaw, "The Devil's Disciple" (MS of scenes for the film in the British Museum, London, Add. 50643). Costello, *Serpent's Eye,* p. 29, dates the scenario for the opening sequence of *The Devil's Disciple* as "in the late 1930's." In an appendix, pp. 163–64, he prints the two scenes between George III and Lord North, and between Lord Germain and his secretary. He does not print the opening sequence.

by States? Colonies are not States: they are parts of my State. Crumbs of it. Crumbs. What do you mean by New England? Where is it? Is it an island? Is it Robinson Crusoe's island? I never heard of it." North shows him New England on a map.

> GEORGE III: What what? North America. Columbus's discovery. Let me see. Let me see. America *is* important, you know, North, quite important. Let me see. (Looking at map) Thats a devilish big place, you know, North. Devilish big. I had no idea it was so big.
>
> LORD NORTH: Very big, sir; and all this side of it is in rebellion.
>
> GEORGE III: What what! Rebellion. Gone Jacobite! Has that drunken blackguard the Pretender broken out again?
>
> LORD NORTH: They never heard of the Pretender, sir. They are dissatisfied.
>
> GEORGE III: Damn their impudence! What about?

North then describes the military situation and explains the plan, in which Generals Howe and Burgoyne are to effect a junction and cut off the rebels. The King dismisses him. The following scene dramatizes what, in the play, General Burgoyne narrates. Lord Germain, impatient to go to the country for the weekend, instructs his secretary to have the order to General Howe ready for his signature "when I return on Tuesday—er—Wednesday."

In the additional scenes for both *Arms and the Man* and *The Devil's Disciple*, Shaw uses visual devices alone, where visual devices can make the dramatic point: e.g., the fugitive Bluntschli climbing onto Raina's terrace, the signing of the Declaration of Independence, and the replacement of the union jack by the American flag. But the camera can go only so far. At a certain point words are necessary to convey information. Cecil Lewis' scenario of *Arms and the Man* [15] begins with the battle of Slivnitza. In the margin beside Lewis' description of what the

---

[15] Cecil Lewis, "Arms and the Man" (MS of the scenario in the Berg Collection, New York Public Library). When I saw the film *Arms and the Man*, the battle scene was missing—as was Bluntschli's explanation concerning the wrong ammunition. This bad print may have been cut by distributors (a practice which is not uncommon: some prints of *Major Barbara*, for example, do not contain a scene which takes place in Albert Hall). Shaw's statement to audiences about to see the film—see above, footnote 13—is probably con-

camera sees, Shaw writes, "It needs dialogue. 'Are those d—d fools going to charge us?' 'Impossible: not a man or a horse will get within thirty yards of it.' 'Cavalry on machine guns! we shall blow them to hell!' 'They must be mad.' 'No: theyre only Bulgarians: they know no better. Be ready: theyre going to do it. Hurry up that ammunition there.' " Where Lewis indicates only that the camera shows the machine gunners frantically pulling at their cartridge belts to find that they do not fit the machine guns, Shaw writes: "This is not intelligible. You must have the incident of the *sergeant* coming in a ghastly fright to Bluntschli. 'Theyve sent us the wrong cartridges, sir.' 'My God: we're done. Run for it, everybody.' Stampede of Servian [*sic*] guns overtaken by the charge."

Were the two early films good? Shaw said yes; most critics said no. Since the public agreed with the critics, British International refused to consider other movie versions of Shaw's plays. If Shaw's assessment is wrong, was he to blame for the failure?

Partly, for his screenplays inadequately adapted the plays to the new medium. *How He Lied to Her Husband* was not, in fact, adapted at all. Except for insignificant variations of a few lines, stage play and screenplay are identical. In the screenplay of *Arms and the Man,* however, Shaw tried to adapt the play to and utilize the possibilities of the film medium. He removed dialogue and stage directions made unnecessary by the camera's selective focus. When Raina takes Petkoff's coat from Nicola and brings it to her father, Shaw the playwright disposes of the servant by having Raina order him to put more wood on the fire. Shaw the screenwriter omits Raina's command, for the camera disposes of Nicola by cutting from a shot of him and Raina to a shot of Raina and Petkoff. Other deletions result in more direct exchanges of dialogue, such as:

PETKOFF: . . . Raina is accustomed to a very comfortable establishment. Sergius keeps twenty horses.

---

clusive evidence that the scene was filmed and, at least on that occasion, shown. Blanche Patch, who was Shaw's secretary, states not only that scene was filmed but that it was filmed in Wales (*Thirty Years with G.B.S.* [London: Gollancz, 1951], p. 122) .

[[BLUNTSCHLI: But who wants twenty horses? We're not going to keep a circus.

CATHERINE (*severely*): My daughter, sir, is accustomed to a first-rate stable.

RAINA: Hush, mother: youre making me ridiculous.]] *

BLUNTSCHLI: Oh well, if it comes to a question of establishment, here goes.[16]

On some occasions, Shaw removes references that a mass, world-wide film audience might not understand, such as Raina's allusion to the opera *Ernani*.

While Shaw preserves the play's major theme—the exposure of romantic illusions of love and war—he badly weakens the secondary theme of class antagonisms. Nicola's warning that if Louka quarrels with the family he cannot marry her since he is dependent on their good will when he opens a shop, his advice that if she tells about the fugitive the Petkoffs would not only discharge her but prevent her from securing another position and evict her father from his farm, his lesson on how to make people believe she is a lady, Sergius' discourse on how soldiers from the lower classes assist the officers in keeping themselves subdued—these and similar speeches are expunged, thereby reducing the play's social issues to the merest resonances as the triangle of Nicola, Louka, and Sergius becomes little more than a variation on the Cinderella theme. Nicola's statement that his engagement to Louka was nominal, designed only to protect her, is changed from toadyism to literal truth.

Shaw's efforts at adaptation include addition as well as subtraction. Unfortunately, most of the new scenes—the flight of Bluntschli, his arrival by horse to return Petkoff's coat, Catherine's replacing the coat in the closet, and others—are brief interruptions of continuing actions which, when we return to these continuing actions in the same or more or less the same location, help to remind us that we are watching a filmed play.

Although Shaw's fledgling screenplays are largely unsuccessful, part of the blame for the failure of both movies must also go to

---

* Double brackets indicate deletions.

[16] Bernard Shaw, *Plays Pleasant and Unpleasant* (London: Constable, 1957), II, 69-70.

their director, Cecil Lewis. In both films the actors usually per-
form in too "big" a manner for the screen, giving the impression
of overplaying. The blocking is stagey—frequent use of cross-and-
turn, and of characters standing and talking to each other. On
some occasions the camera work is trite, for example, Raina,
alone in her room, looks at the bed, whereupon the sleeping
Bluntschli suddenly appears and then disappears.

Lewis does not exploit the film medium as fully as he might
have. Comic capital could have been made by a judicious use of
reaction shots: e.g., Catherine's response when Sergius describes
the mother of Bluntschli's benefactress as an *old* lady. In both
films the camera and editing provide changes from one area of
the setting to the other, but although the camera is not static it is
impartial. In *How He Lied to Her Husband,* for instance, instead of contrasting long shots of the romantic poet with medium
shots and close-ups of the more realistic wife, Lewis merely has a
series of different kinds of long and medium shots, usually of
both characters at the same time. In *Arms and the Man,*
Bluntschli and Raina are framed together at the film's end, but
since they had been framed together throughout the scene the
closing shot has little impact. The director, moreover, fails to
take advantage of cinematic implications in the plays. Shaw
notes, for example, in *How He Lied,* that when the wife leaves
her husband and lover together, *"Bompas deliberately takes the
poems from his breast pocket; looks at them reflectively; then
looks at Henry, mutely inviting his attention. Henry refuses to
understand, doing his best to look unconcerned."* [17] By using
different camera setups, and by appropriate editing, Lewis could
have created a comically suspenseful moment. He might have cut
from a medium shot of the husband examining the poems to a
close-up of the poet refusing to understand, and then to a long
shot of both, the poet trying to look unconcerned. Instead, he
merely showed, in one shot, Bompas reflectively examining the
poems and looking at Henry.

It could be objected, in the case of *How He Lied to Her
Husband,* that there are obvious difficulties in filming a one-set

---

[17] Shaw, *How He Lied to Her Husband,* p. 194.

play without adding new scenes. Although this is certainly true, these difficulties are not insurmountable. Nor is a film which takes place entirely or almost entirely in a single room intrinsically "uncinematic." Once the decision is made to photograph a one-act stage play intact, the transformation from stage to film is the responsibility of the director, who can make this change through the actors, the camera, and the editing. Cecil Lewis failed to accomplish the transformation from one medium to the other.

Three years after the first showing of *Arms and the Man*, Gabriel Pascal arrived upon the scene, apparently charming everyone in the Shaw household and certainly obtaining concessions from Shaw that no one else had been able to obtain. Pascal relates that he arrived at Shaw's flat in Whitehall Court, told him he was the materialization of Dick Dudgeon, proclaimed himself disciple to the bearded dramatist, and requested motion picture rights to *Pygmalion*. Shaw refused. Pascal visited Shaw several times thereafter. Although they became friendly, the playwright hedged. On December 8, 1935, Pascal delivered an ultimatum: unless Shaw gave him the rights by 4:00 P.M. five days later—Friday, the thirteenth—he would leave England to make films in China. That Friday, Pascal waited nervously in his Duke Street flat. At 3:45 he packed his toothbrush. As Big Ben started to strike four, a messenger rang the doorbell. At the fourth stroke, he handed Pascal an envelope containing the contract for *Pygmalion*.[18] Or so Pascal maintains.

Actually, Shaw and Pascal were not the only major figures in the making of *Pygmalion*. Pascal confined himself to producing; Anthony Asquith and Leslie Howard directed. Shaw probably did not secure the control he demanded, for he shared screen credits with three others—a sure sign that changes had been made. While the dialogue is listed as his, the "adaptation" is the work of Cecil Lewis, W. P. Lipscomb, and Ian Dalrymple. Shaw's

[18] Gabriel Pascal, "Shaw as a Scenario Writer," in *G.B.S. 90*, ed. S. Winsten (New York: Dodd, Mead, 1946), pp. 259–60.

published Screen Version is far different from the actual sound track.[19]

The most significant change is the ending, in which Liza returns to Higgins. Whoever was responsible for the new ending, Shaw clearly was not. He learned of it only when he saw the film at a sneak preview. Until that time, he imagined there would be an additional scene showing Liza and Freddy in their flower shop, which he describes in a postscript to the play. At the sneak preview, Pascal was nervous, for he expected Shaw to be angry when he saw the ending. Valerie Delacorte (Pascal's widow) reports that although Shaw was silent after the film ended, there was a faint smile upon his face.[20] While she implies that the smile was one of pleasure, one wonders whether it might not have been wearily ironic. In either case, Shaw did not disown the film. He claimed credit for its success and accepted the Academy Award for the best screenplay of 1938.

But how can the film be said to have dialogue only by Shaw and at the same time have an ending he did not write? Following the play's final scene (Mrs. Higgins' drawing room), the film shows Higgins returning to his Wimpole Street flat. Alone in his laboratory, he accidentally switches on the record player, from which we hear a recording of Liza's voice. Liza then returns, repeating her second act assertion that she washed her hands and face before she came. Higgins, realizing that the voice has come not from the machine but from Liza herself, smiles, and paraphrases his fourth act query about his slippers. The dialogue,

---

[19] The Screen Version consists of the play plus film interpolations, and is printed in many editions, including the Standard (London: Constable, 1957). Costello, *Serpent's Eye*, pp. 165–88, prints the final act of *Pygmalion* in three forms: Play Version, Printed Screen Version, and Sound Track Version. For the first he uses the 1930 Ayot St. Lawrence Edition of Shaw's works. Many of the changes in the published screen version are also found in the revised version of the play which Shaw made for the Standard Edition (1931). Costello's valuable textual comparison is, so far as I know, the only published version of the film's final scenes. Since he covers this film so well, and since it is not entirely Shaw's, I will not devote as much attention to it as to Shaw's other films.

[20] Valerie Delacorte, "GBS in Filmland," *Esquire*, LXII (December, 1964), 288.

therefore, while technically Shaw's, is considerably "adapted" by Lewis, Lipscomb, or Dalrymple.

Except for the ending, the film is faithful to the play. The dialogue does not give way to irrelevant visualizations, and the additional scenes, with the exception noted, derive from suggestions in the play. These new scenes show a Covent Garden crowd (including Liza, Higgins, and Pickering) before the storm, Liza's home after the cabdriver has deposited her there, Higgins demonstrating his equipment to Pickering, Liza going screaming into the steaming bathtub, Higgins giving her lessons, her triumph at the ball, Freddy meeting and kissing her after she leaves Higgins, and Higgins' attempts to find her when he learns of her disappearance.

Since the total running time of *Pygmalion* is eighty-five minutes, and the new scenes occupy thirty-one and one-half minutes,[21] it is obvious that a great deal was cut. Some of the cuts were made because of the added scenes. We are not told about Liza's triumph at the ball, for we see it. Mrs. Higgins and the Maid do not discuss Higgins' dealings with the police, for we see these dealings. Other changes were made in deference to the assumed prurience of moviegoers. Higgins no longer says "Damn," and Liza is no longer called a slut. Doolittle does not mention that he is not married to the woman he is living with, and is not on his way to his own wedding at the end of the play. Other cuts minimize the play's social issues. References to Liza as representative of her class are deleted. Doolittle's role is cut severely, including his "middle-class morality" speech in the fifth act. The Liza-Higgins debate, also in the fifth act, is drastically cut. Much of the Eynsford Hill exposition is gone.

The additions and deletions strengthen the romantic aspect and weaken the social aspect. One reason for *Pygmalion*'s success is not that such changes necessarily result in a good motion picture, but that *Pygmalion* is able to withstand them, for the cuttings do not eliminate the social aspect: they merely make it less explicit. Nor do they remove the plot parallels: Doolittle, like Liza, still moves from one social class to another; the Eyns-

[21] Costello, *Serpent's Eye,* p. 68.

ford Hills, like Liza, are still bred to a way of life they cannot afford.

Major Barbara, a more complex play, suffered greatly when Shaw adapted it to the screen. Departing from his film theories, he drastically altered the play, cutting it to 121 minutes, including 31½ minutes of new scenes,[22] with the camera replacing more than four fifths of the dialogue in Act III, Scene ii.

One recalls Shaw's numerous strictures against cutting. "In a true republic of art," he proclaimed in 1896, "Sir Henry Irving would ere this have expiated his acting versions on the scaffold. He does not merely cut plays: he disembowels them." He compared Irving's vivisection of Shakespeare to the shortening of "one of Velasquez's Philips into a kitcat to make it fit over his drawing room mantelpiece." [23] Yet, almost a half-century later, Shaw himself disemboweled one of his major works—not to hang over a mantelpiece but to be projected on a screen. One can only speculate as to the reasons, but Gabriel Pascal's comment on the adaptation—which Blanche Patch repeats—contains a curious phrase. Shaw, they said, wrote sixteen new scenes for the film, of which Pascal, "for lack of screen time," could use only six.[24] Unlike today's films, which often last three or more hours, movies in the late 1930's and early 1940's usually ran about an hour and a half. If a film ran much more than two hours, it was considered long. To have filmed Shaw's Screen Version of *Major Barbara,* which he later published,[25] would have resulted in a movie of almost four hours, with at least one intermission. Perhaps this consideration persuaded Shaw to make extensive cuts. Whatever his reasons, he made them. The differences between the actual film and the play, as well as the film and the published Screen Version, are enormous. In order to understand the deletions, it is necessary to examine the play.

[22] *Ibid.,* p. 107.

[23] Review of Irving's production of *Cymbeline, Saturday Review,* September 26, 1896. In *Our Theatres in the Nineties* (London: Constable, 1954), II, 197–98.

[24] Pascal, "Shaw as Scenario Writer," p. 257; Patch, *Thirty Years,* p. 127.

[25] Penguin Books first published the Screen Version in England in 1945 and in the United States in 1951. Both editions are out of print. Quotations from the film are from the sound track.

Major Barbara has three focal characters: Undershaft, Cusins, and Barbara. The relative strength of each character has been discussed by numerous critics, who disagree.[26] Undershaft dominates much of the play by his audacity, his wit, his persuasiveness, and the sheer bulk of his role: he has more lines than anyone else. Cusins, too, is important: he wins the pot of gold and marries the heroine; not only does his succession to the firm constitute a major development in the drama, but this intellectual who will make armaments is the potential embodiment of Shaw's Platonic ideal of the philosopher-king. Barbara is also prominent. The play's title predisposes one to regard her as its central figure, and the plot substantiates this, for she initiates and concludes the action. In the first act she suggests to her father that they exchange visits to each other's place of business. The remainder of the play follows this plan. He converts her to his doctrine of realism and power, but she proposes to convert his accomplishments to her own end, salvation. Although the plot hinges chiefly on Barbara, the conception of a single focal character and an uncluttered line of action is too simple to be of much use in exploring so complex a drama. The play blends religion and political economy. Barbara repeats Christ's last words on the cross in the second act and is *"transfigured,"* going "right up into the skies" in the third. Undershaft, urging the destruction of poverty, demonstrates and explains the economic fabric of society. Cusins realizes that the intellectual is ineffectual until he has the power to use his knowledge. These themes are connected, and all three characters are prominent.

Major Barbara is neither tidy nor compartmentalized. Emphasis and focus are split. The play begins in anticipation of Undershaft's arrival: Lady Britomart describes him to her son Stephen and announces his imminent arrival. Once he arrives, he is the center of attention. Barbara becomes very important in the second act, but for most of the third act she is virtually silent

---

[26] E.g., favoring Undershaft: William Irvine, *The Universe of G.B.S.* (New York: Whittlesey House, 1954); favoring Cusins: Charles Frankel, "Efficient Power and Inefficient Virtue," in *Great Moral Dilemmas in Literature, Past and Present,* ed. R. M. MacIver (New York: Harper, 1956); favoring Barbara: Desmond MacCarthy, *Shaw* (London: MacGibbon and Kee, 1951).

while Undershaft delivers long speeches and while he and Cusins haggle first over the latter's qualifications and then over the price of Cusins' joining the firm. Nevertheless, she dominates the play's crucial final scene. After Undershaft leaves the stage, she and Cusins, in reverse order, explain their decisions and goals to each other. A director's difficulty in emphasizing Barbara at the end of Act III is that Shaw has so strongly emphasized Undershaft (and Cusins, too, to an extent) earlier. His difficulty in de-emphasizing her earlier is that she is important here. The shared emphasis, one of the play's special qualities, aids the dialectic and increases the complexity.

Once the decision is made to cut the play for filming, the next decision centers upon emphasis and focus, for this determines what shall be cut. Shaw weakened Undershaft and strengthened Barbara. Because of this decision, a great deal of the social criticism and diabolonian ethics disappeared. In Act I, Undershaft's description of himself as "a profiteer in mutilation and murder" was cut. Lomax does not suggest that "the more destructive war becomes, the sooner it will be abolished" and Undershaft does not reply, "The more destructive war becomes the more fascinating we find it." Nor does he explain,

> I am not one of those men who keep their morals and their business in watertight compartments. All the spare money my trade rivals spend on hospitals, cathedrals, and other receptacles for conscience money, I devote to experiments and researches in improved methods of destroying life and property. I have always done so; and I always shall. Therefore your Christmas card moralities of peace on earth and goodwill among men are of no use to me. Your Christianity, which enjoins you to resist not evil, and to turn the other cheek, would make me a bankrupt. My morality—my religion —must have a place for cannons and torpedoes in it.

Undershaft's third act references to "tricks of the governing class," his use of the government to keep his dividends up and those of his competitors down, the seven deadly sins, the crime of poverty—all, and more, are cut. In place of "The Gospel of St. Andrew Undershaft" are a cinematic montage of the factory and tepid descriptions of what we see. When Undershaft dares Cusins to make war on war, we do not know what he is talking about. In the play, Cusins' decision to join Undershaft is a problem of bridging "an abyss of moral horror." Both the abyss and the phrase are missing from the film, where the problem has become that of an intellectual who is unsure whether he should go into trade.

Since the film emphasizes religion, the second act—which is the religious core of the play—suffers least from cuts. It has, moreover, two substantial additions: Bill Walker's encounter with Todger Fairmile while the latter conducts a Salvation Army meeting, and a huge Salvation Army meeting at Albert Hall (changed from the play's smaller Assembly Hall in the Mile End Road). The beginning of the film focuses on Barbara and religion, rather than on Undershaft and economics. The movie does not open in Lady Britomart's library, but in a park where Cusins is lecturing on ancient Greece. Music from a Salvation Army band interrupts him and lures away his small audience by the promise of livelier entertainment. Cusins gives up and, at the suggestion of a friendly policeman, goes off to hear Barbara preach a long sermon about God. When Barbara asks for converts, Cusins raises his hand. Once they are alone, she inquires about the new happiness that has just entered his life. Candidly confessing that it is not the same happiness that she imagines, he promises to don the Salvation Army uniform, beat the drum, and pursue her until she agrees to marry him. She then takes him home to meet her family, warning that God has some surprises for him. None of these scenes concerning Cusins and Barbara is in the play.

The film's opening scenes emphasize religion and romance rather than Undershaft's morality and the dependence of the aristocracy and the government upon capitalism. Its closing scenes, to a much greater extent than the play, emphasize religion and romance. Cusins no longer explains in detail the reasons for his joining the firm, no longer vows that he will arm the common man against those who exploit him, forcing them to use their genius for the general good. He simply tells Barbara that he will accept her father's offer, and asks whether all is over between them. While her speeches are severely truncated, they are not—like Undershaft's or Cusins'—eliminated. She still says, "I have got rid of the bribe of bread. I have got rid of the bribe of heaven. Let God's work be done for its own sake: the work he had to create us to do because it cannot be done except by living men and women." She and Cusins go off hand in hand, get caught up in a crowd of factory workers, and are joined by Bill Walker, who is now happily working for Undershaft.

Although most of the new scenes are appropriate—Snobby's encounter with his bullying mother, Bill's encounter with Todger Fairmile, Cusins getting drunk in Undershaft's flat—the impact of the film is vastly different from that of the play. The play is a dialectical network of political economy, religion, and the dilemma of the intellectual. The movie is about a religious girl whose fiancé gets a good job with her father's firm.

In addition to the simplification of the social and ethical issues, several minor elements are removed. Exit the Platonic paraphrase ("society cannot be saved until either the Professors of Greek take to making gunpowder, or else the makers of gunpowder become Professors of Greek") and, with it, some of the symbolic significance of Cusins' succession to the firm. References to Dionysos are removed, minimizing the mythic parallels. There are no suggestions of Cusins converting the Salvation Army to the worship of Dionysos, or of Dionysos making him drunk though Undershaft provided the wine. Cusins' cry, "Dionysos Undershaft has descended. I am possessed" is changed to "Saint Undershaft and Saint Bodger have descended—the patron saints of peace and temperance." Philistine moviegoers are not offended, for Lomax' assertion that "there is a certain amount of tosh about the Salvation Army" is cut, and Bill Walker's reference to the red-haired Mog as a "carroty slat" (slut) is purified to "carroty cat."

In brief, Shaw's film adaptation drastically simplified the play. The Shaw-Pascal collaboration did what Shaw feared Hollywood might do.

Their third venture, the second in which only they wrote and directed, and their first in Technicolor, was *Caesar and Cleopatra*. Compared to *Major Barbara*, there was little tampering with the play. *Caesar and Cleopatra*'s 128 minutes contained only 13½ minutes of new scenes.[27]

[27] Costello, *Serpent's Eye*, p. 135.

The additions include a view of Caesar's camp as he walks from his tent into the desert on his way to the Sphinx, Roman troops occupying Alexandria, Caesar working late at night, Cleopatra reluctantly taking a bath and refusing cosmetics when Ftatateeta tells her that Caesar hates perfumes and will not kiss her lips if she reddens them with rouge. Many cuts are made because of added scenes. We do not hear descriptions of what we see: e.g., the efficiency of Roman occupation troops and the burning of the ships in the Alexandrian harbor. Other excisions simplify thought and character: some of Caesar's philosophical statements are deleted, most of Apollodorus' gallantry and comments on art are cut, and all of Ftatateeta's scene in the prologue is removed. Nevertheless, the main line of development—Caesar's efforts to teach Cleopatra to rule without vengeance—remains. This movie, unlike *Barbara,* is faithful to the play.

But most critics agree that the film is unsuccessful. One reason is Shaw, who was eighty-seven to eighty-nine years old during the writing and filming. One can scarcely expect creative vitality from a man that age. As he candidly admitted before his ninety-second birthday, "I can hardly walk through my garden without a tumble or two; and it seems out of all reason to believe that a man who cannot do a simple thing like that can practise the craft of Shakespeare." [28] On July 23, 1944, three days before Shaw's eighty-eighth birthday, Pascal asked him for a new scene to inform the audience that six months pass between Acts III and IV (a stage direction does the job in the text, and a program note accomplishes the task for a production). It is not surprising that Shaw was unable to muster enthusiasm for the project. It took a year for the scene to arrive: a long dialogue in a barber shop, leading to a joke about Rufio refusing to have his beard cut off (the time lapse is mentioned during the conversation).[29] Since the actor playing Rufio was no longer available when the scene was ready to be filmed, Pascal used Shaw's alternate suggestion, a

[28] Bernard Shaw, Preface (1947) to *Buoyant Billions.* In *Buoyant Billions, Farfetched Fables, & Shakes Verses Shav* (New York: Dodd, Mead, 1948), p. 3.

[29] The scene is printed in Marjorie Deans, *Meeting at the Sphinx: Gabriel Pascal's Production of Bernard Shaw's Caesar and Cleopatra* (London: Macdonald, n.d.), and Costello, *Serpent's Eye,* pp. 132–34.

brief scene of a girl harpist and an old musician approaching the palace.

The difficulties encountered during production constitute another reason for the movie's inadequacy. Two months of air raids and V-2 bombings interrupted the shooting schedule and nearly killed several members of the production unit. The war caused delays in transportation and postal communications; shortages of trained technicians and property, scenery, and costume makers; delays in getting material. Pascal rearranged the shooting schedule when he learned that Vivien Leigh (Cleopatra) was pregnant, then rearranged it again after she had a miscarriage. He and Claude Rains (Caesar) did not get along, and at times they were not on speaking terms. The sun refused to shine—a catastrophe for a film planning so much outdoor footage. Pascal then transported the entire production unit to sunny Egypt, where skies were unaccountably gray. With such problems the goal often became one of getting something, no matter how makeshift, on film.

But a third reason for the film's failure is that Pascal directed. Most of the actors lacked verve; all have given better performances under the guidance of other directors. Pascal mistakenly gave the important role of Apollodorus to the muscular Stewart Granger, who is a capable actor but who was terribly miscast as the aesthete whose clothes are *"the most delicate purples and dove greys, with ornaments of bronze, oxydized silver, and stones of jade and agate,"* whose sword rests in *"an openwork scabbard of purple leather and filagree,"* and who proclaims, "I do not keep a shop. Mine is a temple of the arts. I am a worshipper of beauty. My calling is to choose beautiful things for beautiful queens. My motto is Art for Art's sake." [30]

Despite its financial and critical failure, *Caesar and Cleopatra* seems ideal for the screen. The play has many spectacular scenes: an old Syrian palace, a statue of the Sphinx in the middle of the desert, the throne room in Cleopatra's palace, the council chamber in the Alexandrian palace, the quay in front of that palace, the lighthouse in the harbor of Alexandria, Cleopatra's boudoir,

[30] Bernard Shaw, *Three Plays for Puritans* (London: Constable, 1952), pp. 137–38.

the roof of the palace, the harbor where Caesar is about to embark. There are, as well, opportunities to create connecting scenes and to bring in offstage action. Even the play's stage directions, notes Marjorie Deans (Pascal's scenario editor for the film), often read "very much like a film-script." She cites as example the transition from the Syrian palace to the scene before the Sphinx. The earlier scene ends with a mob in general panic. Then, *"The torch is thrown down and extinguished in the rush. The noise of the fugitives dies away. Darkness and dead silence."* The new scene begins with darkness and silence.

> *Then the blackness and stillness break softly into silver mist and strange airs as the wind-swept harp of Memnon plays at the dawning of the moon. It rises full over the desert; and a vast horizon comes into relief, broken by a huge shape which soon reveals itself in the spreading radiance as a Sphinx pedestalled on the sands.*

"What is this," she asks, "but a singularly poetic description of a fade-out, both of sound and picture, from one scene, and of a fade-in to the next?" She also cites the change from the Sphinx to the Throne Room Scene. Caesar follows Cleopatra,

> *the bucina sounding louder as they steal across the desert. The moonlight wanes: the horizon again shews black against the sky, broken only by the fantastic silhouette of the Sphinx. The sky itself vanishes in darkness, from which there is no relief until the gleam of a distant torch falls on great Egyptian pillars supporting the roof of a majestic corridor. At the further end of this corridor a Nubian slave appears carrying the torch. Caesar, still led by Cleopatra, follows him. They come down the corridor, Caesar peering keenly about at the strange architecture, and at the pillar shadows beneath which, as the passing torch makes them hurry noiselessly backwards, figures of men with wings and hawks' heads, and vast black marble cats, seem to flit in and out of ambush.*

This transition, she points out, "is described in terms more obviously fitted to the technique of the screen than of the stage. . . ."[31]

[31] Deans, *Meeting at the Sphinx*, p. 47; Shaw, *Three Plays for Puritans*, pp. 100–101, 107.

Unfortunately, Pascal realized few of these filmic possibilities. The scene in which Caesar follows Cleopatra through the corridors had little of the mystery and excitement of the description. It lacked atmosphere, for Pascal's camera did not explore and his lighting did not reveal. Apollodorus' journey with his royal passenger enclosed in a carpet could have been more interesting than a twenty-second [32] shot of a boat moving away from the harbor. Pascal did not make *Caesar and Cleopatra* visually spectacular: he merely had large settings (but failed to let his camera take advantage of them). Battle scenes and scenes involving troops and crowds were unexciting and even stagey. The cutting did not provide smooth transitions or help build climaxes. Pascal's lack of filmic imagination is demonstrated in a scene which he added to Shaw's script: a montage lasting one minute and forty-five seconds. We see desert battles, victorious Romans pursuing Egyptians, and then what Costello calls "a mystical series of shots showing Caesar alone in the desert with the Sphinx. As Caesar approaches the Sphinx, to the accompaniment of weird, haunting music, he prayerfully echoes his earlier speech: 'For I am he of whose genius you are the symbol: part brute, part woman, and part god.' A hollow voice, apparently from the Sphinx, answers droningly: 'Hail, Caesar!' " [33] Although we do not know Shaw's opinion of these clichés, which tend to give the distorted impression that Caesar's greatness consists primarily of his generalship, Shaw was, according to his biographer Stephen Winsten, unhappy with the film: ". . . it seemed to him that Pascal had turned it into a dull, prosaic, illustrated history." [34]

Major Barbara, also directed by Pascal, has similar faults. The camera is not used imaginatively. The film cutting and camera angles rarely underscore or comment ironically on the action. Instead, Pascal lingers where no lingering is necessary. When Undershaft is going to sign a check for the Salvation Army, a great deal of time is taken with putting on his eyeglasses, re-

[32] Costello, *Serpent's Eye,* p. 131.

[33] *Ibid.,* p. 135.

[34] Stephen Winsten, *Jesting Apostle: The Private Life of Bernard Shaw* (New York: Dutton, 1957), pp. 204–5.

moving his pen, unscrewing the cap, and so forth. Although the aim is apparently suspense, the result is the reverse, for Undershaft merely takes a long time doing what we know he will do. The pace drops, for the play stops. Pascal's lack of inventiveness with stage business is typified in the scene before Lady Britomart's private interview with Undershaft. Since Morrison has announced to her that Undershaft is waiting in the library, Pascal needs a brief transition before they meet. He therefore has Undershaft pick up a photograph and stick out his tongue at it—a childishly petulant action that may derive from Undershaft's remark, "it is only the big men who can be treated as children." Since Undershaft does *not* say, "it is only the big men who *act* like children," and since Shaw describes him as a man with *"formidable reserves of power,"* whose *"gentleness is partly that of a strong man who has learnt by experience that his natural grip hurts ordinary people unless he handles them very carefully, and partly the mellowness of age and success,"* the business is singularly inappropriate. While the original idea may have been Robert Morley's, who played Undershaft, the responsibility was Pascal's, who kept the business in the film.

Pygmalion, in contrast, was not directed by Pascal. Many of the Asquith-Howard directorial touches are equally fitting for the stage—for example, Liza stymied when she finds a plate in one hand and a teacup in the other. Some touches are intensifications of stage devices—e.g., bewildered or shocked faces (in close-up) as Liza describes, with precise diction, her father ladling gin down her mother's throat. Other touches are purely cinematic. When Higgins remembers that he saw the Eynsford Hills at Covent Garden, the film has him whispering the locale to himself while they speak. If he were to do this on the stage, one or both lines would not be understood. The camera shoots from low angles or high angles to indicate dominance or submissiveness. It frames Liza and Higgins, or it separates them by cross-cutting, to show sympathetic or unsympathetic relationships. And, as Costello points out,[35] Asquith and Howard use the camera to match the mood of the character being photographed. When Higgins restlessly paces, the camera also moves and paces

[35] Costello, *Serpent's Eye,* p. 69.

—sometimes to the point of blurring the image—as it tries to keep up with him.

To conclude briefly, the combination of good screenplay and good directing helped make *Pygmalion* a success. The combination of bad screenplay and bad directing, primarily the former, was largely responsible for the failure of *Major Barbara*. Bad directing was mainly responsible for the failure of *Caesar and Cleopatra*.

Shaw's screenplay of *Saint Joan,* written between the filming of *Arms and the Man* and *Pygmalion,* was completed between 1934 and 1936. Periodically, a production was announced. On one occasion, Elisabeth Bergner (who created the role in Germany in 1924) was to play Joan; [36] on another, Wendy Hiller.[37] Granville Barker was once asked to play the Inquisitor.[38] When Greta Garbo was suggested for Joan, however, Shaw vetoed the idea, comparing Garbo as a saint to Mae West as the Virgin Mary.[39] Despite all these possibilities, the project never materialized in Shaw's lifetime; but in 1957, seven years after Shaw's death, Otto Preminger produced and directed a motion picture version of *Saint Joan,* using a screenplay by Graham Greene.[40]

[36] *"Saint Joan* Banned: Film Censorship in the United States," in *Shaw on Theatre,* p. 244.

[37] Langner, *G.B.S. and the Lunatic,* p. 228.

[38] Hesketh Pearson, *G.B.S.: A Postscript* (New York: Harper, 1950), p. 115.

[39] Delacorte, "GBS in Filmland," p. 288.

[40] The cast of this film includes Jean Seberg (Joan), Sir John Gielgud (Warwick), Richard Widmark (the Dauphin), Harry Andrews (De Stogumber), and Richard Todd (Dunois). In a telephone conversation (January 14, 1967), Preminger told me that he was entirely unaware of the existence of Shaw's screenplay, that he did not know that Shaw had written a screen version of *Joan.* Graham Greene's screenplay begins in the bedroom of Charles VII (the Dauphin), the scene of the play's Epilogue, where Joan appears to Charles as he sleeps. Charles begins to reminisce, prompting a flashback to the Baudricourt Scene (i in the play). The film then continues in the same sequence as the play, except that after the scene following the coronation (v), we return to Charles's bedroom where Warwick is introduced, and the heavily cut Tent Scene (iv) is moved to the middle of the Trial Scene (vi). Some of the changes made by Graham Greene, who is Catholic, support

The British Museum contains two versions of the *Saint Joan* screenplay,[41] which I have identified as earlier and later on the basis of both internal and external evidence. The earlier version contains long sections of stage directions and character descriptions taken verbatim from the play, as if a scissors-and-paste job had interlaced the new scenes with the play version. Many long speeches (e.g., the Inquisitor's speech on mercy and justice) are carried verbatim into this screenplay. The later version has more cuts and more cinematic detail. Another copy of the earlier version (identified on the basis of the opening—see Appendix C) is dated October 15, 1934, at the beginning and November 13, 1934, at the end.[42] The later version is undated. On February 15, 1935, Shaw told Lawrence Langner that he had made a scenario of *Saint Joan* for Elisabeth Bergner.[43] The reference may be to either the earlier or later version. On September 14, 1936, a letter by Shaw appeared in *The New York Times,* attacking a censor's prohibition of the filming of *Saint Joan* and

---

the Catholic Church's (rather than Shaw's) view of Joan's trial: that the Church hierarchy was neither actually nor by extension party to the unfair proceedings of Joan's judges (in the play, these judges clearly represent the entire Church). After the court accepts Joan's recantation, Greene adds dialogue in which De Stogumber begs Warwick not to blame the Church but instead to blame the particular French priests who conducted the trial (the absolution and blame therefore remain attached to the same respective parties when the court later finds Joan guilty), and Warwick consoles the English priest with the statement (also not in the play) that Joan will burn before the Pope hears of the matter.

Besides absolving the Pope and the Church hierarchy from any guilt, Greene removes the secular interpretation of one of Joan's miracles. In Scene ii of the play we are told that a besotted, swearing soldier named Foul Mouthed Frank was advised by Joan that he should not swear when at the point of death, following which admonition he drunkenly fell down a well and drowned. Greene's screenplay includes a Frank who is lecherous rather than drunken or foulmouthed. As he passionately reaches for Joan, she remarks that he will soon die. No sooner is this said than Frank, with hands upraised, stiffens and dies, as if felled by a divine hand.

[41] Bernard Shaw, "Saint Joan" (MSS of screenplays in the British Museum, London, Add. 50634).

[42] Letter to Bernard F. Dukore from Miss M. E. Barber, Society of Authors, February 19, 1965.

[43] Langner, *G.B.S. and the Lunatic,* p. 225.

quoting his comments in the margin of the screenplay (later version) .[44]

As early as *Mrs. Warren's Profession* (1894), censorship had prevented performances of Shaw's works. In 1909 he appeared before the Joint Select Committee of the House of Lords and the House of Commons, which had convened to examine the issue of the censorship of stage plays. He urged abolition of censorship and declared that a play should not be suppressed because it might offend the religious feelings of a large part of the community. He replied affirmatively when asked whether ridicule of sacred personages or attacks upon religion should be permitted on the stage, for "the danger of crippling thought, the danger of obstructing the formation of the public mind by specially suppressing such representation is far greater than any real danger that there is from such representations." The real difficulty, he pointed out, "is not to suppress such representations, but, on the contrary, to bring them about," for producers are reluctant to invest money in a play which is contrary to the opinions of a large number of people. Shaw did not mean that the playwright should be exempt from public control; he meant only that he should be exempt from censorship. He would still be answerable to the law.[45]

Shaw's attitude toward censorship did not change with the rise of the motion pictures. In a BBC talk on film censorship on January 20, 1935, he stated categorically, "The censorship method . . . is that of handing the job [of guarding public morals] over to some frail and erring mortal man, and making him omnipotent on the assumption that his official status will make him infallible and omniscient. . . ." [46] In September, 1936, he announced that his plans for making a film of *Saint Joan* had been opposed by Catholic censors.

[44] Reprinted as *"Saint Joan* Banned: Film Censorship in the United States," in *Shaw on Theatre,* pp. 243–52.

[45] Extract of the Minutes of the Joint Committee, reprinted as *Shaw on Censorship,* Shavian Tract No. 3 (London: The Shaw Society, 1955), pp. 2, 6-8.

[46] "Film Censorship," in *Platform and Pulpit,* ed. Dan H. Laurence (New York: Hill and Wang, 1961), p. 262.

A copy of the *Saint Joan* screenplay was sent to the Hollywood censorship bureau, the so-called Hays Office, which, Shaw later learned, included "a body called the Catholic Action, professing, on what authority I know not, to be a Roman Catholic doctrinal censorship." He had, he believed,

> nothing to fear from Catholics who understand the conditions imposed on history by stage representation and are experts in Catholic history and teaching; but as hardly one per cent of Catholics can answer to this description, I have everything to fear from meddling by amateur Busybodies who do not know that the work of censorship requires any qualification beyond Catholic baptism. And the Catholic Action turns out to be a body of just such conceited amateurs.

He reported many of the corrections they demanded: that Cauchon's "the Church cannot take life" be changed to "The Church does not wish death"; that such words as "damned," "St Denis," and "infernal" be deleted; that the scene wherein Joan is "spared the customary torture . . . be omitted from the film, not because it is not true, but because it is 'essentially damaging.'" Because of the censorship, Elisabeth Bergner, who was to play Joan, "is to be seen everywhere on the screen as Catherine of Russia, Empress of Freethinkers and Free Lovers, but may not make the world fall in love with a Catholic saint as she did when she created the part of Joan in Protestant Berlin when my play was new." He called the censor's demands "absurdities" which "represent, not the wisdom of the Catholic Church, but the desperation of a minor official's attempts to reduce that wisdom to an office routine." [47] Shaw's quotations and paraphrases of the censor's objections are wholly accurate. By coincidence, the copy of the *Saint Joan* screenplay in the British Museum files is the copy on which the censor wrote his objections. Appendix B shows the proposed changes and deletions.

In adapting *Saint Joan* to the screen, Shaw may be said to follow the Inquisitor's advice (cut from the screenplay) when he explains his reduction of the indictment from sixty-four counts to twelve: ". . . if we persist in trying The Maid on trumpery issues

---

[47] "*Saint Joan* Banned," pp. 244–46, 248, 250–51.

. . . she may escape us on the great main issue. . . ." [48] The main issue—the destruction, by the combined powers of church and state, of the advanced individual whose actions and statements threaten the religious and political *status quo*—is rigidly adhered to. While Shaw deletes Cauchon's and Warwick's references to Joan as a forerunner of Protestantism and nationalism (Scene iv is cut by more than half), he does not delete the actions and statements that reveal her Protestantism and nationalism. In other words, he removes only the explicit statement. This is his practice throughout. We see it in De Stogumber's description (Epilogue) of his change:

> DE STOGUMBER: I tell my folks they must be very careful. I say to them, "If you only saw what you think about you would think quite differently about it. It would give you a great shock. [[Oh, a great shock.]]" * And they all say "Yes, parson: we all know you are a kind man, and would not harm a fly." That is a great comfort to me. For [[I am not cruel by nature, you know.
>
> THE SOLDIER: Who said you were?
>
> DE STOGUMBER: Well, you see,]] I did a very cruel thing once [in the screenplay, "for once I did a very cruel thing"] because I did not know what cruelty was like. I had not seen it, you know. That is the great thing: you must see it. And then you are redeemed and saved.
>
> [[CAUCHON: Were not the sufferings of our Lord Christ enough for you?
>
> DE STOGUMBER: No. Oh no: not at all. I had seen them in pictures, and read of them in books, and been greatly moved by them, as I thought. But it was no use: it was not our Lord that re-deemed me, but a young woman whom I saw actually burned to death. It was dreadful: oh, most dreadful. But it saved me. I have been a different man ever since, though a little astray in my wits sometimes.
>
> CAUCHON: Must then a Christ perish in torment in every age to save those that have no imagination?]]
>
> JOAN: Well, if I saved all those he would have been cruel to if he had not been cruel to me, I was not burnt for nothing, was I?

[48] All quotations from the play *Saint Joan* are from the Standard Edition (London: Constable, 1961).

* Double brackets indicate deletions.

While we may lament the excisions, their substance is implicit in what remains. In attempting to separate the relevant from the essential, Shaw reduces the Inquisitor's speech (Scene vi) from seventy-eight lines to thirty-six. The historic background of the Inquisition is deleted and its theoretical justification reduced in size. Uncut is the admonition to the court, which is the major purpose of the speech.

Replies are more direct, each line of development moving uninterruptedly—without digression or repetition—toward its climax. In Scene ii, for example:

CHARLES: Why doesnt he [Dunois] raise the siege, then?
LA HIRE: [[The wind is against him.
BLUEBEARD: How can the wind hurt him at Orleans? It is not on the Channel.
LA HIRE: It is on the river Loire; and]] the English hold the bridge-head. He must ship his men across the river and upstream, if he is to take them in the rear. Well, he cannot, because there is a devil of a wind blowing the other way.

In Scene vi:

D'ESTIVET: Why did you jump from the tower?
[[JOAN: How do you know that I jumped?
D'ESTIVET: You were found lying in the moat. Why did you leave the tower?]]
JOAN: Why would anybody leave a prison if they could get out?

An interesting but expendable resonance is discarded: after De Stogumber declares that he would burn Joan with his own hands, Cauchon says, "(*blessing him*) Sancta simplicitas!" (Scene iv) — the words Jan Hus is supposed to have said in 1415 (only sixteen years before Joan was burnt) when he saw a man zealously adding another stick of wood to the pyre on which he was being burnt.

What Shaw keeps is as revealing as what he cuts. Lines and actions demonstrating the principal themes are retained, those demonstrating minor themes removed. Since the responses of De Stogumber and Warwick when Cauchon compares Talbot to a mad bull are comparatively unimportant, both the reference and the responses are cut (Scene iv), but Cauchon's subsequent lines

—"The Church cannot take life. And my first duty is to seek this girl's salvation."—are vital to Shaw's point that Cauchon was acting honorably from his own point of view, and so they remain. Cauchon's statement that his disinterment is a blow against justice, faith, and the very foundations of the Church, constitutes a minor theme and is therefore deleted, but his proximate avowal that he was just, merciful, and faithful to his light (Epilogue) is a major theme and is kept. The "trumpery issue" of the Bishop of Senlis' horse is cut, but Joan's illness from eating carp remains (Scene vi), for it demonstrates that Cauchon is not willingly unkind to her. While the explicit statements that Joan is a forerunner of Protestantism and nationalism are separate from the main action, and therefore dispensable, the Epilogue is essential to Shaw's theme, for in that scene we not only see that it takes centuries for the value of the advanced individual to be recognized, but that even when it is recognized, her actual presence would be disturbing. However, the Saint from Hell, an extraordinary dramatic idea, and relevant as well (he is the only member of Joan's contemporaries from the ranks of the common people), is dispensed with—partly because we have seen him at the execution and partly because he is not essential to the principal dramatic point: the glorification but ultimate rejection of Joan.

In *Saint Joan*'s transition from stage play to film script, complexities are simplified and subtleties excised. The Dauphin is far less cowardly, for such remarks as "I want to be in a comfortable bed, and not live in continual terror of being killed or wounded" (Scene ii) are removed, thus making his peace-loving nature more purely a matter of principle. Joan's statements that she will never take a husband and does not want to be regarded as a woman (Scene iii) are cut, thereby removing psychological complexities. Religious subtleties are also deleted: e.g., the Archbishop's definition of a miracle as an event which, no matter how rational its basis, creates or confirms faith (Scene ii). De Stogumber's anti-Semitism ("I would not leave a Jew alive in Christendom if I had my way"), inessential to any of the major themes, though revelatory of De Stogumber and the type of bigot he represents, is expunged. Warwick's defense of the Jews ("The

Jews generally give value. They make you pay; but they deliver the goods. In my experience the men who want something for nothing are invariably Christians.") is therefore unnecessary and is also cut (Scene iv). Deferring to the supposed prudery of movie audiences, a reference to Charles's mistress Agnes Sorel (Epilogue) is removed.

Not only are many matters simplified, but the social milieu is minimized—possibly on the theory that the camera can show the milieu. Shaw often deletes specific references to feudalism: for example, Baudricourt does not remind Poulengey that as Joan's father's lord he is responsible for her protection (Scene i). Several references to the particular historical epoch are cut, such as (Scene ii):

> THE ARCHBISHOP: . . . There is a new spirit rising in men: we are at the dawn of a wider epoch. If I were a simple monk, and had not to rule men, I should seek peace for my spirits with Aristotle and Pythagoras rather than with the saints and their miracles.
>
> LA TRÉMOUILLE: And who the deuce was Pythagoras?
>
> THE ARCHBISHOP: A sage who held that the earth is round, and that it moves round the sun.
>
> LA TRÉMOUILLE: What an utter fool! Couldnt he use his eyes?

References to Hus and Wycliffe (Scene iv) are struck out, as are Joan's request that her village not be taxed (Scene v) and the Executioner's practice of selling relics after a burning (Scene vi).

Two other excisions might puzzle the spectator who is unfamiliar with the play. Shaw cuts Robert de Baudricourt's explanation of the reference to English soldiers as "goddams" (Scene i):

> ROBERT: Do you know why they are called goddams?
>
> JOAN: No. Everyone calls them goddams.
>
> ROBERT: It is because they are always calling on their God to condemn their souls to perdition. That is what goddam means in their language.

Joan's later use of the term (Scene iii) therefore appears to be an uncharacteristic obscenity, especially since Shaw retains the line that soldiers are reported to have stopped swearing in her presence (Scene i). Another puzzling excision is the Archbishop's account (Scene ii) of why Joan will be able to pick out the Dauphin from the others at court ("She will know what everybody knows: that the Dauphin is the meanest-looking and worst-dressed figure in the Court and that the man with the blue beard is Gilles de Rais"). Without this explanation, and without her explicit identification of Gilles de Rais when she recognizes him —"Coom, Bluebeard" is also cut—this "miracle" lacks a rational basis.

It might seem, at this point, that Shaw's adaptation consists solely of cutting the play. This is not the case. Creating many new scenes that take advantage of the greater resources of film, he enlarges and enriches many aspects of the play. Before Joan dons armor, we watch the effect on her of soldiers marching by. We observe her face as she hears the voices through the ringing of the angelus. Many new scenes dramatize and expand suggestions in the play. Striking scenes of the battle of Orleans and the death of Glasdale supplant descriptions of these events. Joan's military prowess is demonstrated rather than reported: she displays her marksmanship in firing a cannon, and she orders Dunois to blow up the Loire Bridge, a tactic which he and D'Alençon (a character not in the play) admit they would not have thought of. We see rather than hear descriptions of Joan's miraculous recovery after she is wounded, Charles's coronation, Joan's execution, and so forth. A vague suggestion in the play (Scene iv) is expanded to become a new "miracle," which is both awesome and rationally explained: the death of the archer whose arrow struck Joan. Since Salisbury has the archers interrupt their firing in order to reward the marksman who he thinks killed Joan, the French are able to penetrate the English defenses, killing the archer and Salisbury as the latter is bestowing the reward. The spectacular additional scenes, all in harmony with the original play, transcend the physical limits of stage representation.

Taking advantage of the cinema's greater scenic resources, Shaw not only adds new scenes but changes scenes which he retains from the stage version. Instead of going from the Tent Scene to the Cathedral Scene (iv to v), Shaw exploits the film medium to show simultaneous action as he cuts from the tent to the coronation in Rheims Cathedral, back to the tent, then to the ambulatory in the cathedral, and then to the Archbishop's palace. Characters are no longer confined to a single set within each scene but roam freely about the castle: e.g., Baudricourt and Poulengey (Scene i). In short, the film medium is fully exploited.

In *Saint Joan*'s transition from stage to screen, scenes from the play are streamlined, while new scenes extend the action and broaden the scope. Although something has been lost in *Joan*'s adaptation, a great deal has been gained, for Shaw attempted to utilize the techniques of the new medium in presenting a film version of his play. His success may be seen in the following pages. The *Joan* screenplay is important partly because it was *not* filmed. A director neither improved it nor ruined it: the pages that follow are, for better or for worse, pure Shaw. They may serve as a model of how he wanted his plays to be filmed.

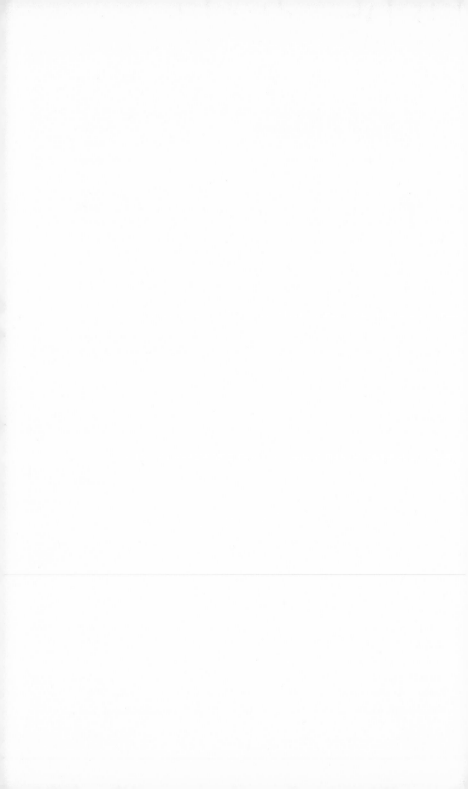

Editor's Note

THE TYPESCRIPT of Shaw's screenplay of *Saint Joan* does not consistently use his idiosyncratic punctuation (e.g., *dont* for *don't*), spelling (*shew* for *show*), and emphasis (spaces between letters, instead of italics). Where it does not, I have altered it to conform to Shaw's usage.

I am grateful to the Public Trustee and the Society of Authors for permission to quote from Shaw's writings, published and unpublished, and to print his screenplay of *Saint Joan*. Acknowledgment is also made to the Henry W. and Albert A. Berg Collection of the New York Public Library, Astor, Lenox, and Tilden Foundations for permission to publish the passages from the corrected typescript of the scenario of *Arms and the Man*. I am grateful to John Ehmann, editor of the University of Notre Dame Press, for generously making available galley proofs of Donald P. Costello's *The Serpent's Eye: Shaw and the Cinema* while I was preparing my manuscript. I also thank the staff of the British Museum and both John D. Gordan and Mrs. Charles Szladits of the Berg Collection for their help.

For arranging a showing of *How He Lied to Her Husband* and *Arms and the Man*, I would like to thank Margareta Akermark of the Museum of Modern Art and Colin Ford of the British Film Institute. I would also like to thank Otto Preminger for allowing me to examine Graham Greene's screenplay of *Saint Joan,* which he directed, and Mrs. Bernice Stavis for arranging a showing of this film.

For photographs of various productions of *Saint Joan*, my thanks go to the following persons and institutions (listed alphabetically by country): AUSTRALIA—S. James of the Adelaide *Advertiser;* E. H. Medlin of the University of Adelaide. ENGLAND—Angus McBean; The National Theatre; *Plays and Players;* Dame Sybil Thorndike. FINLAND—Mrs. Arja Seimola of the

Helsinki Theatre Museum. FRANCE—Mme. J. Colomb-Gérard; Jacques Guignard of the Arsenal Library. GERMANY—Rolf Badenhausen of the Institute for Theatre Scholarship of the University of Cologne. IRELAND—*The Connacht Tribune*. JAPAN —Masahiko Masumoto; Mrs. Vera Scriabine of the New York Shavians, Inc. THE NETHERLANDS—Karel Muller of the Toneelgroep Theater; Erik Vos; Max Wagener of the Netherlands Center of the International Theatre Institute. POLAND—Miss Olga Axer of *Poland;* Antoni Debnicki of the Theatre Section of the Polish Art Institute; Mrs. Aldona Pruchnicka of the Polish Center of the International Theatre Institute. RUSSIA—Mme. L. Bykovskaja of the Moscow Central Theatre Library; Daniel C. Gerould of San Francisco State College. SWEDEN—G. Campbell-Westlind, Deputy Consul General in New York; Harry G. Carlson of Queens College; Torsten Henriksson of the Swedish Institute for Cultural Relations. SWITZERLAND—Myron Gubitz. UNITED STATES—Lincoln Center Library of the Performing Arts of the New York Public Library; The Minnesota Theatre Company Foundation; Michael Wager. YUGOSLAVIA—Darko Suvin.

I am greatly indebted to Professor Sidney P. Albert, of California State College at Los Angeles, with whom I spent many hours discussing *Major Barbara* and who helped me considerably in interpreting the play. For his help in understanding film technique, I am most grateful to Lawrence Dukore, film editor.

Finally, but foremost, I especially want to thank Professor Ruby Cohn, of San Francisco State College, for her invaluable suggestions during the preparation of this manuscript.

Saint Joan

A SCREENPLAY
BY
BERNARD SHAW

THE lights in the auditorium are faded out.

Peals of bells as from many church towers, high and low notes increasing in intensity. Appears on the screen the main title of the film:

SAINT JOAN

The sound of the bells gradually diminishing provides a background to the subsequent subtitles, fading out entirely at the end of the last subtitle: Time: the years 1429–1431.[1] Pastures near Domrémy. The edge of a cliff overlooking a vast plain. A church tower rises from a clump of trees. A burnt out farmhouse, still smouldering, in the middle distance. Sheep browsing.

JOAN is sitting on the grass with her hands clasped round her ankles, gazing intently at the burnt house. Her shepherd's crook is beside her. Also her sheep dog.

[1] In an earlier draft, Shaw wrote a slightly different opening. See Appendix C.

Her back is to the audience.

A marching song is heard, very distant, soldiers singing and drums marking time.

Rum tum trumpledum,
Bacon fat and rumpledum,
Old Saint mumpledum,
Pull his tail and stumpledum
    O my Ma-ry-Ann!

JOAN rises to her knees, and shades her eyes with her hand, listening and looking for the source of the sound.

She flings out her arm, waving to the soldiers, and marks time with her feet.

The dog, puzzled by these proceedings, and fearing something wrong with her, noses or paws at her anxiously.

She turns round and sits down, caressing the dog, reassuringly, and shewing her face to the audience for the first time.

The angelus is rung in the church tower.

JOAN rises and stands at attention, like a soldier, but with clasped hands, and radiant face.

Her expression changes to one of intense determination. She snatches up her crook and

strides down the hill, leaving
the dog to look after her sheep.

Fade in

A stone chamber on the first
floor of the Castle of Vaucouleurs. The morning sun.

CAPTAIN ROBERT DE BAUDRI-
COURT, a military squire, handsome and physically energetic,
is seated at a well-provisioned
breakfast table. His STEWARD
stands facing him.

ROBERT
No eggs! Thousand thunders,
man, what do you mean by no
eggs?

STEWARD
Sir: it is not my fault. It is the
act of God.

ROBERT
You blame your Maker for it.

STEWARD
Sir: what can I do? I cannot lay
eggs.

ROBERT (*Sarcastic*)
Ha! You jest about it.

STEWARD
No, sir, God knows. We all have
to go without eggs, just as you
have, sir. The hens will not lay.

5

ROBERT

Indeed!

(*Rising*)

My three Barbary hens and the black are the best layers in Champagne. And you tell me that there are no eggs!

(*Driving the Steward to the wall*)

Who stole them? The milk was short yesterday, too.

STEWARD (*Desperate*)

No, sir: nobody will steal anything. But there is a spell on us: we are bewitched.

ROBERT

That story is not good enough for me. Robert de Baudricourt burns witches and hangs thieves. Go. Bring me four dozen eggs and two gallons of milk before noon, or Heaven have mercy on your bones!

He resumes his seat with an air of finality.

STEWARD

Sir, I tell you there will be no eggs—not if you were to kill me for it—as long as The Maid is at the door.

ROBERT

The Maid! What Maid?

STEWARD

The girl from Lorraine, sir. From Domrémy.

ROBERT (*Rising in fearful wrath*)

Thirty thousand thunders! Fifty thousand devils! Do you mean to say that that girl who had the impudence to ask to see me two days ago is here still?

STEWARD

I have told her to go, sir. She wont.

ROBERT

I did not tell you to tell her to go: I told you to throw her out. You have fifty men-at-arms and a dozen lumps of able-bodied servants to carry out my orders. Are they afraid of her?

STEWARD

She is so positive, sir.

ROBERT (*Seizing him by the scruff of the neck*)

You parcel of curs: you are afraid of her.

STEWARD (*Hanging limp in his hands*)

No, sir: we are afraid of you; but she puts courage into us. She really doesnt seem to be afraid of anything. Perhaps you could frighten her, sir.

ROBERT (*Grimly*)

Perhaps. Where is she now?

STEWARD

Down in the courtyard, talking to the soldiers as usual. She is always talking to the soldiers, except when she is praying.

ROBERT

Praying, you idiot? I know the sort of girl that is always talking to soldiers. She shall talk to me a bit.

With these words he turns towards the spiral staircase and walks out of the picture. The STEWARD follows.

Cut to

A view of the courtyard, it is a sunny day in early spring. The snow is melting, dripping from the roofs; cocks crow, cows low; at intervals the clanging of hammer blows from a smithy can be heard. A few cannons, no longer in service, stand in a corner; birds sing. Far in the background a group of soldiers can be seen through a wooden grille; they are seated and in their midst appears a figure in light garb, apparently a girl.

ROBERT (*Stopping at the doorstep, shouts fiercely*)
Hallo, you there!

A GIRL'S VOICE (*Bright, strong and rough*)
Is it me, sir?

ROBERT
Yes, you.

VOICE
Be you captain?

ROBERT
Yes,—damn your impudence.
Come here.
(*To the soldiers*)
Shove her along, quick!

The girl dashes through the
wooden gate into the courtyard, splashing through pools
of water . . . straight towards
ROBERT.

STEWARD (*Edging into the pic-
ture, whispering*)
She wants to be a soldier herself.
She wants you to give her soldiers'
clothes. Armor, sir, and a sword!
Actually.

He steals behind ROBERT.

JOAN (*Bobbing a curtsey*)
Good morning, Captain squire.
Captain: you are to give me a
horse and armor and some soldiers and send me to the Dauphin. Those are your orders from
my Lord.

ROBERT
Orders from y o u r lord? And
who the devil is your lord?

JOAN
My Lord is the King of Heaven.

ROBERT

Why, the girl's mad.
(*To the Steward*)
Why didnt you tell me so, you
blockhead?

STEWARD

Sir: do not anger her: give her
what she wants.

JOAN

Squire, it is the will of God that
you are to do what He has put
into my mind.

ROBERT

It is the will of God that I shall
send you back to your father with
orders to put you under lock and
key and thrash the madness out
of you.

JOAN

You think you will, squire; but
you will find it all coming quite
different. You said you would not
see me; but here I am.

STEWARD (*Appealing*)

Yes, sir. You see, sir.

ROBERT

Hold your tongue!

STEWARD (*Abjectly*)

Yes, sir.

ROBERT (*To Joan, with a sour loss of confidence*)

So you are presuming on my seeing you, are you?

JOAN (*Sweetly*)

Yes, squire.

ROBERT (*Feeling that he has lost ground, inflates his chest imposingly to cure the unwelcome and only too familiar sensation*)

I am going to assert myself.

JOAN (*Busily*)

Please do, squire. The horse will cost sixteen francs. It is a good deal of money: but I can save it on the armor. I am very hardy; and I do not need beautiful armor made to my measure like you wear. I shall not want many soldiers: the Dauphin will give me all I need to raise the seige of Orleans.

ROBERT (*Flabbergasted*)

To raise the seige of Orleans?

JOAN (*Simply*)

Yes, squire: that is what God is sending me to do. Three men will be enough for you to send with me. They have already promised to come with me. Polly and Jack and—

ROBERT

Polly? you impudent baggage, do
you dare call Squire Bertrand de
Poulengey, Polly to my face?

JOAN

His friends call him so, squire:
Jack—

ROBERT

That is Monsieur John of Metz,
I suppose.

JOAN

Yes, squire. Jack will come willingly. So will Dick the Archer
and their servants, John of Hone-
court and Julian. There will be
no trouble for you, squire: I have
arranged it all: you have only to
give the order.

ROBERT (*Contemplating her in
a stupor of amazement*)
Well, I am damned!

JOAN (*With unruffled sweet-
ness*)
No, squire: God is very merciful:
and the blessed Saints Catherine
and Margaret, who speak to me
every day—

He gapes.

—will intercede for you. You will
go to Paradise; and your name
will be remembered for ever as
my first helper.

ROBERT (*To the Steward, still much bothered, but changing his tone as he pursues a new clue*)
Is this true about Monsieur de Poulengey?

STEWARD (*Eagerly*)
Yes, sir.

ROBERT (*Thoughtful*)
Mf!

Camera pans to the other side of the hall where one sees a well kept courtyard.

ROBERT (*Shouts to a passing soldier*)
Hallo! Send Monsieur de Poulengey to me, will you?
(*He turns to Joan*)
Wait in the yard.

JOAN (*Smiling brightly at him*)
Right, squire.

She goes out.

STEWARD (*Anxious that the matter should go on*)
Sir, think of those hens, the best layers in Champagne; and—

ROBERT
Think of my boot; and take your backside out of reach of it.

The STEWARD retreats hastily.

From the other side—from the courtyard—appears:

13

BERTRAND DE POULENGEY, a French gentleman-at-arms, aged thirty-six or there about, employed in the department of the provost-marshal, dreamily absent-minded, speaking slowly and obstinate in reply: altogether in contrast to the self-assertive, loud-mouthed, talkative, energetic, but fundamentally will-less ROBERT.

POULENGEY salutes and stands awaiting orders.

ROBERT (*Genially*)
It isnt service, Polly. Its about the girl you are interested in. First, she's mad. That doesnt matter. Second, I know her class. Her father is a farmer. He might have a cousin a lawyer, or in the Church. People of this sort can give a lot of bother to the authorities. That is to say, to me. Now no doubt it seems to you a very simple thing to take this girl away, humbugging her into the belief that you are taking her to the Dauphin. But if you get her into trouble, you may get me into no end of a mess. So, Polly, hands off her.

POULENGEY (*With deliberate impressiveness*)
I should as soon think of the Blessed Virgin herself in that way, as of this girl.

ROBERT

You are not going to tell me that you take her crazy notion of going to the Dauphin seriously, are you?

POULENGEY (*Slowly*)

There is something about her. They are pretty foulmouthed in the guardroom, some of them. But there hasnt been a word that has anything to do with her being a woman. They have stopped swearing before her. There is something. Something. It may be worth trying.

ROBERT

Oh, come, Polly! Pull yourself together.

He accompanies him up the spiral stairs. The camera follows. (During the following dialogue they stop occasionally, talking, then proceed again, etc.)

ROBERT

Commonsense was never your strong point: but this is a little too much.

POULENGEY (*Unmoved*)

What is the good of commonsense? If we had any commonsense we should join the Duke of Burgundy and the English king. They hold half the country, right down to the Loire. They have Paris. The Dauphin is in Chinon,

15

like a rat in a corner. We dont even know that he is the Dauphin: his mother says he isnt. The Queen denies the legitimacy of her own son.

ROBERT (*Shrugging his shoulders*)
Well, she married her daughter to the English king.

POULENGEY
The English will take Orleans: nothing can save our side now but a miracle.

They are now one or two steps below the entrance to the stone room.

ROBERT
Oh! You think the girl can work miracles, do you?

POULENGEY
Her words and her ardent faith in God have put fire into me.

ROBERT (*Giving him up*)
Whew! You are as mad as she is.

POULENGEY (*Obstinately*)
We want a few mad people now. See where the sane ones have landed us!

They have now arrived at the top, facing the stone room.

ROBERT (*Undecided*)
Do you think I ought to have another talk to her?

Cut to

Corner in the Yard, near the smithy.

The clanging of the hammer can now be plainly heard. JOAN —illuminated by the fire in the smithy—watches how a cannon is being repaired. A few soldiers and the STEWARD stand about her.

POULENGEY'S VOICE
Joan!

Camera pans to POULENGEY leaning out of window on the first floor just above JOAN.

JOAN (*Raising her voice above the hammering in the smithy*)
Will he let us go, Polly?

POULENGEY
Come up.

JOAN brightly winks to the STEWARD, confident of victory. She hurries across the court, the STEWARD following to shew her the way.

The room on the first floor. POULENGEY sits down, ROBERT remains standing to impress his imposing presence.

JOAN enters.

POULENGEY (*Gravely*)
Sit down, Joan.

JOAN (*Checked a little, and looking to Robert*)
May I?

ROBERT
Do what you are told.

JOAN curtsies and sits down on a stool between them. ROBERT outfaces his perplexity with his most peremptory air.

ROBERT
What is your name?

JOAN (*Chattily*)
They always call me Jenny in Lorraine. Here in France I am Joan. The soldiers call me The Maid.

ROBERT
What is your surname?

JOAN
Surname? What is that? My father sometimes calls himself d'Arc; but I know nothing about it.

ROBERT
What did you mean when you said that St Catherine and St Margaret talked to you every day?

JOAN
They do.

ROBERT
What are they like?

JOAN (*Suddenly obstinate*)
I will tell you nothing about that: they have not given me leave.

SWITZERLAND (Zurich, 1951; directed by Joseph Millo, designed by Teo Otto). *Scene i*. Margareth Carl as Joan; left of Joan: Robert Schwarz as Poulengey; right: Leonard Steckel as Baudricourt.

POLAND (Stary Theatre, Cracow, 1956; directed by Władysław Krzeminski; designed by Tadeusz Kantor) . *Scene ii*. Maria Kosciałkowska as Joan.

(Photograph by Vandamm)

UNITED STATES (New York, 1923; directed by Philip Moeller; designed by Raymond Sovey). *Scene i.* Winifred Lenihan as Joan; seated: Ernest Cossart as Baudricourt.

(Photograph by *The Connacht Tribune*)

IRELAND (The Gaelic Theatre, Galway, 1950). *Scene i.* Siobhan McKenna as Joan.

ENGLAND (The National Theatre, Chichester, 1963; directed by John Dexter). *Scene ii.* Joan Plowright as Joan; Robert Stephens as the Dauphin.

SWITZERLAND (Zurich, 1939; directed by Leopold Lindtberg; designed by Teo Otto). *Scene ii.* Maria Becker as Joan; behind Joan: Ernst Ginsberg as the Dauphin.

JAPAN (Tokyo, 1963; directed by Tsuneari Fukuda). *Scene ii.* Kyoko Kishida as Joan; Noboru Nakaya as the Dauphin.

UNITED STATES (New York, 1956; directed by Albert Marre). *Scene ii.* Siobhan McKenna as Joan; Michael Wager as the Dauphin.

GERMANY (Deutsches Theater, Berlin, 1924; directed by Max Reinhardt). *Scene ii.* Elisabeth Bergner as Joan; Rudolf Forster as the Dauphin.

(Photograph by Vandamm)

UNITED STATES (New York, 1936; directed by Guthrie McClintic; designed by Jo Mielziner). *Scene iii.* Katherine Cornell as Joan; left of Joan: Kent Smith as Dunois.

FINLAND (Viipurin Näyttämö Theatre, Viipuri, 1925). *Scene iii.* Emmi Jurkka as Joan.

YUGOSLAVIA (Croatian National Theatre, Zagreb, 1955; directed and designed by Bojan Stupica) . *Scene iii*. Mira Stupica as Joan; left of Joan: A. Ćejvan as Dunois; behind Joan: A. Dulčić as the Page.

ROBERT

But you actually see them; and they talk to you as I am talking to you?

JOAN

No: it is quite different. I cannot tell you: you must not talk to me about my voices.

ROBERT

What do you mean? Voices?

JOAN

I hear voices telling me what to do. They come from God.

ROBERT

They come from your imagination.

JOAN

Of course. That is how the messages of God come to us.

POULENGEY

Checkmate.

ROBERT

No fear!
(To Joan)
So God says you are to raise the siege of Orleans?

JOAN

And to crown the Dauphin in Rheims Cathedral.

ROBERT (*Gasping*)
Crown the D——! Gosh!

JOAN
And to make the English leave France.

ROBERT (*Sarcastic*)
Anything else?

JOAN (*Charming*)
Not just at present, thank you, squire.

ROBERT
I suppose you think raising a siege is as easy as chasing a cow out of a meadow.
(*Grimly*)
Did you ever see English soldiers fighting?

JOAN
They are only men. God made them just like us; but He gave them their own country and their own language; and it is not His will that they should come into our country and try to speak our language.

ROBERT
Who has been putting such nonsense into your head? Dont you know that soldiers are subject to their feudal lord? and that it is nothing to them whether he is the

Duke of Burgundy or the King
of England or the King of France?
What has their language to do
with it?

JOAN

We are all subject to the King of
Heaven and He gave us our coun-
tries and our languages, and
meant us to keep to them. If it
were not so it would be murder
to kill an Englishman in battle;
and you, squire, would be in great
danger of Hell fire. You must not
think about your duty to your
feudal lord, but about your duty
to God.

POULENGEY

It's no use, Robert: she can choke
you like that every time.

ROBERT

Can she! by Saint Denis! We shall
see.
    (*To Joan*)
We are not talking about God:
we are talking about practical af-
fairs. I ask you again, girl, have
you ever seen English soldiers
fighting, plundering, burning?
Have you heard no tales of their
Black Prince, who was blacker
than the devil himself?

JOAN

You must not be afraid, Robert—

ROBERT

Damn you, I am not afraid. And who gave you leave to call me Robert?

JOAN

You were called so in Church in the name of our Lord. All the other names are your father's or your brother's or anybody's.

ROBERT

Tcha!

JOAN (*Rises impetuously, and goes at him, unable to sit quiet any longer*)

Squire, you will live to see the day when there will not be an English soldier on the soil of France; and there will be but one King there; not the feudal English king, but God's French one.

ROBERT (*To Poulengey*)

Rot! . . . But the Dauphin might swallow it. And if she can put fight into him, she can put it into anybody.

POULENGEY

There is something about the girl—

ROBERT (*Turning to Joan*)

Now, listen you to me; and
    (*Desperately*)
dont cut in before I have time to think.

JOAN (*Plumping down on the stool again like an obedient schoolgirl*)
Yes, squire.

ROBERT
Your orders are, that you are to go to Chinon under the escort of this gentleman and three of his friends.

JOAN (*Radiant, clasping her hands*)
Oh, squire! Your head is all circled with light like a saint's.

POULENGEY
How is she to get into the royal presence?

ROBERT (*Who has looked up for his halo rather apprehensively*)
I dont know: how did she get into m y presence? If the Dauphin can keep her out he is a better man than I take him for.

He rises.

JOAN
And the dress? I may have a soldier's dress, maynt I, squire?

ROBERT
Have what you please.

JOAN (*Wildly excited by her success*)
Come, Polly.

She dashes out.

23

ROBERT (*Shaking Poulengey's hand*)
Goodbye, old man, I am taking a big chance. But as you say, there is something about her.

POULENGEY
Yes: there is something about her. Goodbye.

He goes out.

ROBERT, still very doubtful whether he has not been made a fool of by a crazy female, and a social inferior to boot, scratches his head and slowly comes back from the door.

Voice of the STEWARD, shouting.

STEWARD
Sir, sir!

ROBERT
What now?

STEWARD (*Dashes up the spiral stairs; he points to basket full of eggs*)
The hens are laying like mad, sir. Five dozen eggs!

In his excitement he trips over the last step, falling full length into the room. A few eggs smash on the floor.

ROBERT (*Crosses himself, and stammers*)
Christ in Heaven!
(*Aloud but breathless*)
She did come from God.

A close up of ROBERT as he says
these last portentous words.

Slow dissolve

Beautiful, far-flung evening
scenery.

In the distance a number of
horsemen; they appear practically as silhouettes, but their
armor glistens in the rays of
the setting sun.

The horseman in the centre is
noticeably smaller of stature
and slimmer than the others.

Evening bells are heard from
afar; the wind moves the brush-
wood in the foreground.

Slow dissolve

A coat-of-arms hewn in stone
above a portal of the Castle of
Chinon.

Dissolve

A reception room in the castle.
The camera moves down as
from the ceiling of the room,
bringing into focus

   a PAGE

opening the door and announc-
ing:

             PAGE
           The Dauphin.

The following people are waiting for him:

The ARCHBISHOP OF RHEIMS
LA TRÉMOUILLE
LA HIRE and
GILLES DE RAIS.

The ARCHBISHOP, a prelate of imposing bearing close on 50. LA TRÉMOUILLE, a monstrous, arrogant wineskin of a man, GILLES DE RAIS, a young man of 25, very smart and self-possessed, sporting the extravagance of a little curled beard, dyed blue at a clean-shaven Court. He is determined to make himself agreeable, but lacks much natural joyousness, and is not really pleasant. LA HIRE, a war dog with no Court manners and pronounced camp ones. The DAUPHIN, aged 26, really KING CHARLES VII, since the death of his father but as yet uncrowned, enters with a paper in his hands. He is a poor creature physically; and the current fashion of shaving closely, and hiding every scrap of hair under the headdress, both by women and men, makes the worst of his appearance. He has the expression of a young dog accustomed to be kicked, yet incorrigible and irrepressible, but he is neither vulgar nor stupid; and he has a cheeky humor which enables him to hold his own in conversation. Just at present he is excited, like a child with a new toy.

CHARLES

Oh, Archbishop, do you know what Robert de Baudricourt is sending me from Vaucouleurs?

THE ARCHBISHOP

I am not interested in the newest toys.

CHARLES (*Indignantly*)

It isnt a toy.

LA TRÉMOUILLE

It is my business to know what is passing between you and the garrison at Vaucouleurs.

He snatches the paper from the DAUPHIN's hand, and begins reading it with some difficulty, following the words with his finger and spelling them out syllable by syllable.

CHARLES

You all think you can treat me as you please because I owe you money and because I am no good at fighting. But I have the blood royal in my veins.

THE ARCHBISHOP

Even that has been questioned, your Highness. One hardly recognizes in you the grandson of Charles the Wise.

CHARLES

I want to hear no more of my

grandfather. He was so wise that he used up the whole family stock of wisdom for five generations, and left me the poor fool I am, bullied and insulted by all of you.

GILLES DE RAIS and LA HIRE laugh at this without restraint.

THE ARCHBISHOP
Control yourself, sir. These outbursts of petulance are not seemly.

CHARLES
A lecture! Thank you. What a pity it is that though you are an archbishop, saints and angels dont come to see you!

THE ARCHBISHOP
What do you mean?

CHARLES
Aha! Ask that bully there.
(*Pointing to La Trémouille*)

LA TRÉMOUILLE (*Furious*)
Hold your tongue. Do you hear?

CHARLES
Oh, I hear. You neednt shout. Why dont you go and shout at the English? and bully them instead of bullying me?

LA TRÉMOUILLE (*Raising his fist*)
You young—

CHARLES (*Running behind the Archbishop*)
Dont you raise your hand to me. It's high treason.

THE ARCHBISHOP (*Resolutely*)
Come, come! This will not do. My Lord Chamberlain: please! please! we must keep some sort of order.
(*To the Dauphin*)
And you, sir: if you cannot rule your kingdom, at least try to rule yourself.

CHARLES
Another lecture! Thank you.

LA TRÉMOUILLE (*Handing the paper to the Archbishop*)
Here: read the accursed thing for me. He has sent the blood boiling into my head: I cant distinguish the letters.

CHARLES (*Coming back and peering round La Trémouille's shoulder*)
I will read it for you if you like. I can read, you know.

LA TRÉMOUILLE (*With intense contempt; not at all stung by the taunt*)
Yes: reading is about all you are fit for. Can you make it out, Archbishop?

THE ARCHBISHOP

I should have expected more commonsense from de Baudricourt.
He is sending some cracked country lass here—

CHARLES

No: he is sending a saint: an
angel. And she is coming to me:
to me, the King, and not to you,
Archbishop. She knows the blood
royal if you dont.

He struts past GILLES DE RAIS
and LA HIRE.

THE ARCHBISHOP

This creature is not a saint. She
is not even a respectable woman.
She does not wear women's
clothes. She is dressed like a soldier, and rides round the country
with soldiers.

CHARLES

You havnt read the end of the
letter, Archbishop. De Baudricourt says she will raise the siege
of Orleans and beat the English
for us.

LA TRÉMOUILLE

Rot!

GILLES DE RAIS (*Coming between the Archbishop and
Charles*)

At the head of your troops in
Orleans you have the invincible
Dunois, the darling of all the

ladies, the wonderful bastard. Is it likely that a country lass can do what he cannot do?

CHARLES
Why doesnt he raise the siege, then?

LA HIRE
The English hold the bridgehead. He must ship his men across the river and upstream, if he is to take them in the rear. Well, he cannot, because there is a devil of a wind blowing the other way. What he needs is a miracle.

GILLES DE RAIS
We can easily find out whether she is an angel or not. Let us arrange when she comes that I shall be the Dauphin and see whether she will find me out.

CHARLES
Yes: I agree to that. If she cannot find the blood royal I will have nothing to do with her.

Dissolve

Close up of GILLES DE RAIS standing theatrically on the dais before the throne—

Chatter and laughter on all sides. . . .

The camera moves back gradually revealing the entire

throne room. The Court is assembled. GILLES DE RAIS, like the courtiers, enjoying the joke rather obviously. There is a curtained arch in the wall behind the dais: but the main door, guarded by men-at-arms, is at the other side of the room. CHARLES is in the midst of a group of courtiers in the centre of the room. LA HIRE is on his right. The ARCHBISHOP on his left. LA TRÉMOUILLE stands on the dais by the side of the throne. The DUCHESS OF TRÉMOUILLE, surrounded by a group of ladies in waiting, behind the ARCHBISHOP.

The chatter of the courtiers makes such a noise that nobody notices the appearance of the PAGE at the door.

> PAGE
> The Duke of—

Nobody listens.

> PAGE
> The Duke of—

The chatter continues. Indignant at his failure to command a hearing the PAGE snatches the halberd of the nearest man-at-arms, and thumps the floor with it. The chatter ceases and everybody looks at him.

> PAGE
> Attention! The Duke of Vendôme presents Joan the Maid to His Majesty.

CHARLES hides behind the nearest courtier, peering out to see what happens.

JOAN, dressed as a soldier, with her hair bobbed and hanging thickly round her face, is led in by a bashful nobleman, from whom she detaches herself to stop and look round eagerly for the DAUPHIN.

All the ladies explode in uncontrollable laughter.

A titter runs through the Court as she walks to the dais.

JOAN looks at him sceptically for a moment, scanning him hard up and down to make sure. Dead silence, all watching her. Fun dawns in her face.

CHARLES (*Putting his finger on his lip*)
Ssh!

GILLES DE RAIS (*Majestically*)
Let her approach the throne.

THE DUCHESS (*To the nearest lady in waiting*)
My dear! her hair!

GILLES DE RAIS (*Trying not to laugh, and waving his hand in deprecation of their merriment*)
Ssh—ssh! ladies! ladies!!

JOAN (*Not at all embarrassed*)
I wear it like this because I am a soldier. Where be Dauphin?

GILLES DE RAIS (*Condescendingly*)
You are in the presence of the Dauphin.

JOAN
Thou canst not fool me. Where be Dauphin?

A roar of laughter breaks out as GILLES, with a gesture of surrender, joins in the laugh, and jumps down from the dais. JOAN, also on the broad grin, turns back, searching along the row of courtiers, and presently makes a dive, and drags out CHARLES by the arm. Releasing him, she bobs him a little curtsey.

JOAN
Gentle little Dauphin, I am sent to you to drive the English away from Orleans and to crown you king in the Cathedral of Rheims.

CHARLES (*Triumphant, to the Court*)
You see, all of you: she knew the blood royal. Who dare say now that I am not my father's son?
(*To Joan*)
But if you want me to be crowned at Rheims you must go up to the Archbishop, not to me. There he is.

The ARCHBISHOP is standing behind JOAN.

JOAN (*Turning quickly, over-whelmed with emotion*)
Oh, my lord!

She falls on both knees before him, with bowed head, not daring to look up.

34

My lord: you are filled with the glory of God Himself; but you will touch me with your hands and give me your blessing, wont you?

THE ARCHBISHOP (*Touched, putting his hand on her head*)
Child: you are in love with religion.

JOAN (*Startled: looking up at him*)
Am I? I never thought of that. Is there any harm in it?

THE ARCHBISHOP
There is no harm in it, my child. But there is danger.

JOAN rises with the sun-flush of reckless happiness irradiating her face.

JOAN
There is always danger, except in heaven. Oh, it must be a most wonderful thing to be Archbishop.

The Court smiles broadly: even titters a little.

THE ARCHBISHOP (*Drawing himself up sensitively*)
Gentlemen: your levity is rebuked by this maid's faith. I am, God help me, all unworthy; but your mirth is a deadly sin.

Their faces fall. Dead silence.

GILLES DE RAIS
My Lord: we were laughing at her, not at you.

35

The courtiers take heart at this. There is more tittering.

JOAN (*Scandalized*)
You are an idle fellow, and you have great impudence to answer the Archbishop.

LA HIRE (*With a huge chuckle*)
Well said, lass! well said!

JOAN (*Impatiently to the Archbishop*)
Oh, my lord, will you send all these silly folks away so that I may speak to the Dauphin alone?

LA HIRE (*Good humoredly*)
I can take a hint.

He salutes, turns on his heels, and goes out.

THE ARCHBISHOP
Come, gentlemen. The Maid comes with God's blessing and must be obeyed.

The courtiers withdraw, some through the arch, others at the opposite side. The ARCHBISHOP marches across to the door, followed by the DUCHESS and LA TRÉMOUILLE. As the ARCHBISHOP passes JOAN, she falls on her knees, and kisses the hem of his robe fervently. He shakes his head in instinctive remonstrance: gathers the robe from her; and goes out. JOAN is left kneeling directly in the DUCHESS's way.

36

THE DUCHESS (*Coldly*)
Will you allow me to pass, please?

JOAN (*Hastily rising, and standing back*)
Beg pardon, maam, I am sure.

The DUCHESS passes on.

JOAN (*Staring after her: whispers to the Dauphin*)
Be that Queen?

CHARLES
No. She thinks she is.

JOAN (*Again staring after the Duchess*)
Oo-oo-ooh!

Her awe-struck amazement at the figure cut by the magnificently dressed lady is not wholly complimentary.

LA TRÉMOUILLE (*Very surly*)
I'll trouble your Highness not to gibe at my wife.

He goes out. The others have already gone.

JOAN (*To the Dauphin*)
Who be old Gruff-and-Grum?

CHARLES
He is the Duke de la Trémouille.

JOAN
What be his job?

CHARLES
He pretends to command the army. And whenever I find a friend I can care for, he kills him.

JOAN
Why dost let him?

CHARLES moves petulantly to
the throne side of the room to
escape from her magnetic field.

JOAN
Art afraid?

CHARLES
Yes: I am afraid. It's no use
preaching to me about it. It's all
very well for these big men with
their armor that is too heavy for
me and their swords that I can
hardly lift. They like fighting;
but I am quiet and sensible and
only want to be left alone. So if
you are going to say "Son of Saint
Louis: gird on the sword of your
ancestors, and lead us to victory"
you may spare your breath to cool
your porridge; for I am not built
that way; and there is an end of it.

JOAN
I shall put courage into thee.

CHARLES
But I dont want to have courage
put into me. Put courage into the
others, and let them have their
bellyful of fighting; but let me
alone.

JOAN
It's no use, Charlie: if thou fail
to make thyself king, thoult be a
beggar: what else art fit for?

Come! Let me see thee sitting on the throne. I have looked forward to that.

CHARLES

What is the good of sitting on the throne when the other fellows give all the orders? However!

He sits on throne, a piteous figure.

Here is the King for you! Look your fill at the poor devil.

JOAN

Thourt not King yet, Charlie: thourt but the Dauphin. The people will not have a man be king of France until he is crowned in Rheims Cathedral. Thou needs new clothes, Charlie. Why does not Queen look after thee properly?

CHARLES

We're too poor. She wants all the money we can spare to put on her own back.

JOAN

There is some good in thee, Charlie; but it is not yet a king's good.

CHARLES

We shall see. I am not such a fool as I look. I have my eyes open; and I can tell you that one good treaty is worth ten good fights.

These fighting fellows lose all on the treaties that they gain on the fights. If we can only have a treaty, the English are sure to have the worst of it, because they are better at fighting than at thinking.

JOAN

If the English win, it is they that will make the treaty. Thou must fight, Charlie! We must take our courage in both hands: aye, and pray for it with both hands too.

CHARLES descends from his throne and again crosses the room to escape from her dominating urgency.

CHARLES

Oh do stop talking about praying.

JOAN

I have a message to thee from God; and thou must listen to it, though thy heart break with the terror of it.

CHARLES

I dont want a message; but can you tell me any secrets? Can you turn lead into gold, or anything of that sort?

JOAN

I can turn thee into a king, in Rheims Cathedral; and that is a miracle that will take some doing, it seems.

CHARLES
Will the consecration pay off my mortgages? I have pledged my last acre to that fat bully Trémouille.

JOAN
The land is thine to rule righteously, and not to pledge at the pawnshop as a drunken woman pledges her children's clothes. God has sent me to tell thee to kneel in the Cathedral and to become King. The very clay of France will become holy: her soldiers will be the soldiers of God: the rebel dukes will be rebels against God: the English will return to their lawful homes. Wilt be a poor little Judas and betray Him that sent me?

CHARLES (*Tempted at last*)
Oh, if I only dare.

JOAN
I shall dare in God's name! Art for or against me?

CHARLES (*Excited*)
I'll risk it. I warn you I shant be able to keep it up: but I'll risk it. You shall see.

CHARLES runs to the main door and shouts:

CHARLES
Hallo! Come back, everybody.

To JOAN, as he runs back to the arch opposite:

41

Mind you stand by and dont let me be bullied.

(*Shouting through the arch*)

Come along, will you: the whole court!

He sits down in the royal chair as they all hurry in to their former places, chattering and wondering.

Now I am in for it; but no matter: here goes!

(*To the Page*)

Call for silence, you little beast, will you?

PAGE snatches a halberd as before and thumps with it repeatedly:

PAGE

Silence for His Majesty the King. The King speaks.

(*Peremptorily*)

Will you be silent there?

Silence.

CHARLES (*Rising*)

I have given the command of the army to The Maid. The Maid is to do as she likes with it.

General amazement. LA HIRE, delighted, slaps his steel thigh-piece with his gauntlet.

LA TRÉMOUILLE (*Turning threateningly towards Charles*)

What is this? *I* command the army.

JOAN quickly puts her hand on CHARLES's shoulder as he instinctively recoils.

CHARLES, with a grotesque ef-

fort, culminating in an extrav-
agant gesture, snaps his fingers
in the CHAMBERLAIN's face.

Suddenly she flashes out her
sword, divining that her moment has come.

JOAN
Thourt answered, old Gruff-and-
Grum.

Who is for God and His Maid?

Who is for Orleans with me?

LA HIRE (*Carried away, drawing also*)
For God and His Maid! To Orleans!

All the knights, following his
lead, draw their swords shouting:

To Orleans!

JOAN, radiant, falls on her
knees in thanksgiving to God.
They all kneel, except the
ARCHBISHOP, who gives his bene-
diction with a sign, and LA
TRÉMOUILLE, who collapses,
cursing.

The points of the swords

Dissolve to

A pennon fluttering in the east
wind on the banks of the Loire
(during the dissolve one hears
the whistling wind) .

A sudden pan of the camera
brings the face of DUNOIS into

43

focus. He looks upon the pennon and shakes his fist at it, etc.

See below.

(The whole of the following scene, especially the dialogue between DUNOIS and JOAN, must be heroically interpreted by sudden and decisive movements of the camera, increasing in rapidity.)

Over the head of DUNOIS one sees the silver Loire and a wide view beyond the river. In the background the town walls of Orleans, the towers and spires of the city against the evening sky. The pennon flutters from a lance rammed into the ground.

DUNOIS, aged 26. His shield with its bend sinister (the sign of illegitimacy) lies beside the lance. He has his commander's baton in his hand. He is well built, carrying his armor easily.

His broad brow and pointed chin give him an equilaterally triangular face, already marked by active service and responsibility, with the expression of a good natured and capable man who has no affectations and no foolish illusions.

His PAGE is sitting on the ground, elbows on knees, cheeks on fists, idly watching the water.

DUNOIS (*Looks at the pennon, and shakes his fist at it*)
Change, curse you, change, English harlot of a wind, change to the west, I tell you!

With a sigh he makes a few paces in silence, but soon begins again.

DUNOIS
False wind from over the water, will you never blow again? [2]

PAGE (*Bounding to his feet*)
See! There! there she goes!

DUNOIS, startled from his reverie:

DUNOIS (*Eagerly*)
Who? Where? The Maid?

PAGE
No, the kingfisher!

DUNOIS (*Furiously disappointed*)
Is that all? You infernal young idiot: I have a mind to pitch you into the river.

A SENTRY'S VOICE (*Westwards*)
Halt! Who goes there?

JOAN'S VOICE
The Maid!

DUNOIS
Let her pass.

[2] In an earlier draft, this scene began differently. See Appendix D.

JOAN, in splendid armor, rushes
in in a blazing rage.

JOAN (*Bluntly*)
Be you Bastard of Orleans?

DUNOIS (*Cool and stern, point-
ing to the shield*)
You see the bend sinister. Are you
Joan the Maid?

JOAN
Sure.

DUNOIS
Where are your troops?

JOAN
Miles behind. They have cheated
me. They have brought me to the
wrong side of the river.

DUNOIS
I told them to.

JOAN
Why did you? The English are on
the other side!

DUNOIS
The English are on both sides.

JOAN
But Orleans is on the other side.
We must fight the English there.
Which is the way to the bridge?

DUNOIS
You are impatient, Maid.

JOAN

Is this a time for patience? Our enemy is at our gates. Oh, why are you not fighting? I will deliver you from fear, I—

DUNOIS (*Laughing heartily and waving her off*)

No, no, my girl: if you delivered me from fear I should be a good knight for a story book, but a very bad commander of the army. Come! Let me begin to make a soldier of you.

He takes her to the water's edge.

Do you see those two forts at this end of the bridge?

With these words the camera pans, bringing into view the two forts in the distance; little of the bridge comes into focus.

JOAN

Are they ours or the goddams'?

DUNOIS

Be quiet, and listen to me. If I were in either of those forts with only ten men I could hold it against an army. The English have more than ten times ten goddams in those forts to hold them against us.

JOAN

They cannot hold them against God. God did not give them the

47

land under those forts: they stole it from Him. He gave it to us. I will take those forts.

DUNOIS
Single-handed?

JOAN
Our men will take them. I will lead them.

DUNOIS
Not a man will follow you.

JOAN
I will not look back to see whether anyone is following me.

DUNOIS (*Recognizing her mettle, and clapping her heartily on the shoulder*)
Good. You have the makings of a soldier in you. You are in love with war.

JOAN (*Startled*)
Oh! And the Archbishop said I was in love with religion.

DUNOIS
I, God forgive me, am a little in love with war myself, the ugly devil! I am like a man with two wives. Do you want to be like a woman with two husbands?

JOAN
I will never take a husband. A

man in Toul took an action against me for breach of promise; but I never promised him. I am a soldier: Bastard, I dare you to follow me.

DUNOIS

You must not dare a staff officer, Joan: only company officers are allowed to indulge in displays of personal courage. However, all in good time. Our men cannot take those forts by a sally across the bridge. They must come by water, and take the English in the rear on this side.

JOAN (*Her military sense asserting itself*)

Then make rafts and put big guns on them; and let your men cross to us.

DUNOIS

The rafts are ready; and the men are embarked. But they cannot come up against both wind and current. We must wait until God changes the wind. Come: let me take you to the church. You must pray for a west wind. My prayers are not answered. Yours may be.

JOAN

Oh yes: I will pray: I will tell St Catherine: she will make God give me a west wind. Quick: shew me the way to the church.

THE PAGE (*Sneezes violently*)
At-cha!!!

JOAN
God bless you, child! Coom, Bastard.

They go off. The PAGE rises to follow. He picks up the shield, and is taking the spear as well when he notices the pennon, which is now streaming eastward.

THE PAGE (*Dropping the shield and calling excitedly after them*)
Seigneur! Seigneur! Mademoiselle![3]

DUNOIS (*Running back*)
What is it? The kingfisher?

He looks eagerly for it up the river.

JOAN
Oh, a kingfisher! Where?

THE PAGE
No: the wind, the wind, the wind.
(*Pointing to the pennon*)
That is what made me sneeze.

DUNOIS (*Looking at the pennon*)
The wind has changed. God has spoken.

Kneeling, he hands his baton to JOAN.

You command the King's army.

Rises.

---

[3] In an earlier draft, Shaw showed the pennon as the wind changed direction. See Appendix E.

50

You dared me to follow. Dare you lead?

JOAN bursts into tears and flings her arms round DUNOIS, kissing him on both cheeks.

JOAN

Dunois, dear comrade in arms, help me. My eyes are blinded with tears.

DUNOIS (*Dragging her out*)
Make for the flash of the guns.

JOAN (*In a blaze of courage*)
Ah!

DUNOIS (*Dragging her along with him*)
For God and Saint Denis!

THE PAGE (*Shrilly*)
The Maid! The Maid! God and The Maid!

Dissolve to

Cannonade.

The river Loire at Orleans, with the bridge in the distance and the tower, rather like a castle chessman, at the end farthest from the city.

Sound of gunfire and distant shouts.

On a huge raft with a cannon mounted on it JOAN, the DUC D'ALENÇON and DUNOIS stand watching the tower as the raft half drifts, half sails with a big lugsail towards it. The raft is crowded with men-at-arms.

The MASTER GUNNER is laying the cannon. His ASSISTANT stands by with his linstock burning.

JOAN, after looking eagerly from the cannon to the tower and back again at the cannon, pushing the gunner away, says:

Continual din of distant shouting and talking on the raft, but not loud enough to drown JOAN's voice.

JOAN

No, too high, you cant reach it. The shot must bounce up off the water. Let me. Let me.

She lays the cannon herself. Silence on the raft, all watching.

Now, now!

She snatches the linstock and fires the cannon, which is loaded with black powder and makes a thick smoke.

D'ALENÇON

Good shot, Maid. Youve breached the tower.

JOAN (*Exultant*)

I knew I should. I can do that every time. Ah!!

An arrow strikes her in the throat. She screams and falls.

After JOAN's scream, shout of triumph heard from the enemy.

DUNOIS and D'ALENÇON rush to her.

She cries piteously, like a baby.

The GUNNER plucks the arrow away (it has wounded her neck

and stuck in her coat of mail),
eliciting a piercing scream from
her.

Scream from JOAN.

She cries still more piteously.

D'ALENÇON
Those cursed English archers.

DUNOIS
A surgeon there. She will bleed to
death.

JOAN
No. No surgeon. Lift me: I want
to pray.

DUNOIS and D'ALENÇON lift her
to her knees whilst the CAN-
NONEER makes a bandage of
tow to put round her neck.

JOAN clasps her hands in sup-
plication.

JOAN
O blessed Madame Saint Margaret, O dear Madame St Catherine,
do not let me bleed to death. My
work is not done. Oh, you must
not—you will not—

GUNNER
By God, the flow of blood has
stopped. The wound has healed.
Look!

He throws away the bandage.

D'ALENÇON
A miracle! On your knees! God is
on this raft.

The men-at-arms kneel, cross-
ing themselves.

JOAN, smiling in ecstasy and springing to her feet, says:

JOAN
The pain is gone: I have my strength again. Gloria in exelsis Deo. Up, up, up! to work, to work.

The men-at-arms rise and shout defiance at the enemy.

Shouts.

The top of the circular tower against the sky. The battlements are of timber. In the middle is a rough rail round the stairhead into the interior, and a flagstaff with the English standard.

The battlements are manned by English archers, each with his long bow, and his supply of arrows stuck in the battlement beside him.

They stand at an equal distance between each, and shoot rhythmically together in volleys. At each flight, they give the English "Hurrah!" to terrify the French.

FIRST VOLLEY
Hurrah!

They take fresh arrows and draw their bows to the ear.

SECOND VOLLEY
Hurrah!

They notch and draw again.

THIRD VOLLEY
Hurrah!

LORD SALISBURY comes up by the stairs.

54

SALISBURY
Attention!

They turn and stand at attention.

Where is the man whose arrow struck the Maid?

An ARCHER steps forward and salutes, grinning.

SALISBURY, taking a purse from his belt, says:

SALISBURY
You know, all of you, that the Maid is a witch, accurst of God and His saints.

They salute.

You know that the only way to destroy a witch's damnable magic is to draw her blood.

They salute again.

This purse contains ten gold pieces. This man has drawn the blood of the witch: we have nothing to fear now. The gold is his. Take it in God's holy name.

He holds out the purse to the ARCHER.

The highly gratified ARCHER stretches out his hand to take the purse.

A cannon ball splinters a battlement; strikes SALISBURY and the ARCHER down, groaning and mortally wounded, scattering the gold pieces in all directions; and shivers the flagstaff, bringing down the standard.

All stare horror-stricken until the report of the cannon follows.

Report of cannon.

The Archers, panic stricken, lower their heads and rush to the stairs, down which they disappear.

The last ARCHER: that is, the least frightened, is tempted by the gold whilst waiting for the stairs to clear.

He picks up two pieces and looks at them doubtfully.

JOAN's cannon fires another shot.

Sound of cannon.

The ARCHER shudders; flings away the gold; crosses himself, and runs to the stairs.

SALISBURY groans and expires.

The ARCHER is already dead.

Flashes on the screen indicating the fire from shot and shell, but no details are seen.

Then: challenging hurrays—as if in the immediate vicinity—they stop abruptly, as if torn asunder.

Quick fade in

The English archers standing on the battlements of the bridge tower.

As if stricken with paralysis they gaze at

Cut to

THE MAID with a white banner bearing the Holy Names.

Alone, she strides towards the tower, the banner fluttering in the wind.

Curt commands from the tower and a hail of arrows cuts the air. Without hesitation, a host of French soldiers throw themselves into the picture, whipping up their courage with cries of "God and The Maid!" Overtaking the MAID, they storm forward wildly to the attack. More and more men press forward. Trumpet signals, cannon shots, cries.

Dissolve to

The bank near the bridge.

The men-at-arms are leaping ashore.

> D'ALENÇON
> That last shot has cleared the top of the tower. They are on the run.

> DUNOIS
> They will scatter into the country and escape us. We must stop the rout.

57

JOAN

Thoult do nowt of the sort, Jack. If they scatter into the country so much the better for us. The danger is that theyll cross the bridge to take cover in the town. Thou must blow up the bridge.

DUNOIS

Blow up the Loire bridge! Youre mad.

JOAN

A broken bridge is soon mended. Master Gunner: land thy cannon but leave thy powder aboard and bring what more thou canst lay hands on. The rest of you fetch straw and anything that will burn up quickly and heap it over the powder. I want a fireship.

DUNOIS

But what for? What will you do with it?

JOAN

Anchor it under the bridge; set fire to the straw; and get ashore quick as best we can, sink or swim.

THE SOLDIERS (*Jubilant*)

Ay, ay, The Maid is right. Powder there. Straw there. God and The Maid.

Bags of powder and trusses of straw are thrown on board.

JOAN sets to to stack them.

Soldiers jump from the shore back to the raft to help her.

DUNOIS
I should never have thought of that.

D'ALENÇON
Neither should I.

DUNOIS
We are no use here. We must lead the attack on the tower. Come.

He springs ashore and hurries off.

D'ALENÇON
Carry on, Maid. We'll clear out the tower.

The Bridgehead, at the foot of the tower.

English and Burgundian archers (the Burgundian archers have crossbows) in confusion and terror. Some are still pouring out through the tower gate. SIR WILLIAM GLASDALE and a couple of other Knights on horseback arrive and rally them. The movement of the men ceases. They look to him for a lead.

GLASDALE
Steady there, steady. Stand there, will you. All across the bridge, into the town. Follow me.

KNIGHTS
À Glasdale! À Glasdale! Follow up. Across the bridge. This way.

SOLDIERS
À Glasdale! À Glasdale!

They stream off across the bridge.

A big explosion, followed by several minor ones.

Appalling shrieks from the wounded. Cries of terror.

A torrent of fugitives surges back upon the tail of the advance.

FUGITIVES
Fly, fly. Back for your lives. The witch.

AN ENGLISH SERGEANT (*Collaring a fugitive*)
What are we to fly for? Stand up to it, you curs. À Glasdale! À Glasdale! What has frightened you, man?

All stop to listen.

THE FUGITIVE
Hell has opened under Glasdale's feet. He has fallen into the bottomless pit, man and horse and hundreds with him. The witch and all her devils are clawing them. Fly.

SERGEANT (*Releasing him*)
Holy Savior!

He turns and runs.

They all run madly from the bridge.

The top of the tower by moonlight.

60

The two corpses lie where they fell.

JOAN's standard flies from the broken flagstaff.

JOAN, kneeling in prayer, with an expression of intense pity.

D'ALENÇON rushes up the stairway.

D'ALENÇON

What are you doing here? I have been searching for you everywhere.

JOAN

I am praying for the souls of these two poor men.

D'ALENÇON

Pray them into hell, blast them! Dont you see that they are English goddams?

JOAN

Dont be angry with me.

D'ALENÇON

But youve seen hundreds of dead men today. Why need you bother about these two?

JOAN

They looked so lonely. I had to pray for them.

D'ALENÇON

Psha! You must learn when to be

a saint and when to be a soldier; for you cant be both at the same time.

JOAN
But the battle is over; and we have won. God has saved France.[4]

Dissolve to

A sunny day. A beflagged street in Orleans, the town gate in the background. Church bells ringing in victory; a large crowd in the streets, on the roofs, people waving out of the windows. Women, men, children, the aged, all shouting themselves hoarse in jubilant cries of:

"The Maid!"
Riding in the middle of a procession of victorious troops entering the city, mounted on a white charger, impressively bridled,

THE MAID.

She holds the white banner, blackened by the smoke of battle, torn and slashed.

Close up

In contrast to the elaborate harness of her horse, the happy and at the same time shyly

---

[4] In an earlier draft, the scene continued for two more speeches. A scene between De Stogumber and the Cardinal of Winchester followed. See Appendix F.

smiling face of THE MAID, acknowledging the acclamations of the crowd.

This close up of JOAN *dissolves to*

A *close up* of a book with beautiful pictures, a strong, manly hand turning the leaves.

The cries and shouts fade out during the dissolve.

Silence. The camera moves back. . .

A tent (in the English camp). An imposing NOBLEMAN, aged 46, is seated in a handsome chair at a table, turning over the leaves of the illuminated book. At the other side of the table a CHAPLAIN of 50, sitting on a stool, hard at work writing.

During the whole of the following scene the hubbub from the camp at intervals invades the tent. The neighing of horses, the stamping of galloping hooves, shouts, words of command, etc. Rays of the sun illuminate the interior of the tent.

THE NOBLEMAN

Now this is what I call workmanship. There is nothing on earth more exquisite than a bonny book with well placed columns in beautiful borders, and illuminated pictures.

THE CHAPLAIN
I must say, my lord, you take our situation very coolly, very coolly indeed.

THE NOBLEMAN (*Supercilious*)
What is the matter?

THE CHAPLAIN
The matter, my lord, is that we English have been defeated.

THE NOBLEMAN
That happens, you know. It is only in history books and ballads that the enemy is always defeated.

THE CHAPLAIN
But we are being defeated over and over again. Jargeau, Meung, Beaugency, just like Orleans.
(*He throws down his pen*)
By God, if this goes on any longer I will fling my cassock to the devil, and take arms myself, and strangle the accursed witch with my own hands.

THE NOBLEMAN
Easy, man, easy: we shall burn the witch and beat the Bastard all in good time. Indeed I am waiting at present for the Bishop of Beauvais, to arrange the burning with him.

A Page appears. Behind him, outside, a view of the camp, tents, soldiers, etc.

CAUCHON, aged about 60, comes in. The PAGE withdraws. The two Englishmen rise.

THE PAGE
The Right Reverend the Bishop of Beauvais: Monseigneur Cauchon.

THE NOBLEMAN (*With effusive courtesy*)
My dear Bishop, how good of you to come! Allow me to introduce myself: Richard de Bauchamp, Earl of Warwick, at your service.

CAUCHON
Your lordship's fame is well known to me.

WARWICK
This reverend cleric is Master John de Stogumber.

THE CHAPLAIN (*Glibly*)
John Bowyer Spencer Neville de Stogumber, Keeper of the Private Seal to His Eminence the Cardinal of Winchester.

CAUCHON
Messire John de Stogumber: I am always the very good friend of His Eminence.

He extends his hand to the CHAPLAIN, who kisses his ring.

WARWICK
Do me the honor to be seated.

65

He gives CAUCHON his chair, placing it at the head of the table.

CAUCHON accepts the place of honor with a grave inclination. WARWICK fetches another chair carelessly, and sits in his former place. The CHAPLAIN goes back to his chair.

Though WARWICK has taken second place in calculated deference to the BISHOP, he assumes the lead in opening the proceedings as a matter of course. He is still cordial and expansive; but there is a new note in his voice which means that he is coming to business.

WARWICK
Well, my Lord Bishop, you find us in one of our unlucky moments. Charles is to be crowned at Rheims, practically by the young woman from Lorraine.

During these words

Dissolve to

Coronation day in Rheims.

The procession to the cathedral through the mediaeval street. Men-at-arms line the pavements and keep the surging crowd pressed back against the houses. Windows and roofs crowded with sightseers. Priests chanting. Folk shouting and throwing. The procession is

Sounds of Priests chanting and people shouting.

66

headed by CHARLES on horseback with his peers and churchmen. Behind them, a gap in the procession is filled by JOAN carrying her banner on her white horse. After her, a car representing the city of Orleans. Then archers on foot, etc.

The square in front of the cathedral, of course without the equestrian statue of JOAN which now stands there.

Another view of the procession as it enters the cathedral.

tion anthem being sung. The cathedral choir. Corona-   Singing.

CHARLES enthroned in royal robes.

The ARCHBISHOP pours the holy oil on his head from a little vial.

JOAN sits the crown on his head; then falls on her knee and kisses his hand.

Music rises to a climax.

The tent.

WARWICK
I suppose it will make a great difference to Charles's position?

CAUCHON
Undoubtedly. It is a master stroke of The Maid's.

THE CHAPLAIN (*Agitated*)
We were not fairly beaten, my lord. No Englishman is ever fairly beaten.

CAUCHON raises his eyebrows slightly, then quickly composes his face.

WARWICK
Our friend here takes the view that the young woman is a witch. It would, I presume, be the duty of your Reverend Lordship to denounce her to the Inquisition, and have her burnt for that offense.

CAUCHON
I am afraid the bare fact that an English army has been defeated by a French one will not convince them that there is any witchcraft in the matter.

Disappointment on the faces of WARWICK and the CHAPLAIN. . .

CAUCHON
The names on The Maid's white banner are not the names of Satan and Beelzebub, but the blessed names of our Lord and His holy mother.

WARWICK (*Looking very dubious*)
Well, what are we to infer from this, my lord? Has The Maid converted you?

CAUCHON
If she had, my lord, I should have

known better than to have trusted myself herewith in your grasp.

WARWICK
Oh! my lord!

CAUCHON
She is not a witch. She is a heretic!

WARWICK (*Speaking after a moment's thought*)
My lord: I wipe the slate as far as the witchcraft goes. None the less, we must burn the woman.

CAUCHON
The Church cannot take life. And my first duty is to seek this girl's salvation.

WARWICK
No doubt. But you do burn people occasionally.

CAUCHON
No. When the Church cuts off an obstinate heretic as a dead branch from the tree of life, the heretic is handed over to the secular arm. The Church has no part in what the secular arm may see fit to do.

WARWICK
Precisely. And I shall be the secular arm in this case. Well, my lord, hand over your dead branch; and I will see that the fire is ready for it.

CAUCHON

No, my lord: the soul of this village girl is of equal value with yours or your kin's before the throne of God; and if there be a loophole through which this baptized child of God can reach to her salvation, I shall guide her to it.

THE CHAPLAIN (*Rising in a fury*)

You are a traitor.

CAUCHON (*Springing up*)

You lie, priest.

(*Trembling with rage*)

If you dare do what this woman has done—set your country above the holy Catholic Church—you shall go to the fire with her.

THE CHAPLAIN

My lord: I—I went too far. I—

(*He sits down with a submissive gesture*)

WARWICK (*Who has risen apprehensively*)

My lord: I apologize to you for the word used by Messire John de Stogumber. It does not mean in England what it does in France. In your language traitor means betrayer: one who is perfidious, treacherous, unfaithful, disloyal. In our country it means simply one who is not wholly devoted to our English interests.

CAUCHON
I am sorry. I did not understand. *(He subsides into his chair with dignity)*

WARWICK *(Resuming his seat, much relieved)*
I must apologize on my own account if I have seemed to take the burning of this poor girl too lightly. When one has seen whole countrysides burnt over and over again as mere items in military routine, one has to grow a very thick skin. Otherwise one might go mad: at all events, I should.

THE CHAPLAIN
I speak under correction; only this: but The Maid is full of deceit: she pretends to be devout. Her prayers and confessions are endless. How can she be accused of heresy when she neglects no observance of a faithful daughter of The Church?

CAUCHON *(Flaming up)*
A faithful daughter of The Church! The Pope himself at his proudest dare not presume as this woman presumes. She acts as if she herself were The Church. She brings the message of God to Charles; and The Church must stand aside. S h e crowns him in the Cathedral of Rheims. She sends letters to the King of En-

gland, giving him God's command through her own mouth to return to his island on pain of God's vengeance, which she will execute. Has she ever in all her utterances said one word of The Church? Never. It is always God and herself. It is not the Mother of God now to whom we must look for intercession, but to Joan The Maid. What will the world be like when the Church's accumulated wisdom and knowledge and experience, its councils of learned, venerable, pious men, are thrust into the kennel by every ignorant dairymaid? What will it be when every girl thinks herself a Joan? I shudder to the very marrow of my bones when I think of it. If she does not recant in the dust before the world, and submit herself to the last inch of her soul to her Church, to the fire she shall go!

WARWICK obviously considers the result of the conversation to be sufficient for the day. He rises.

WARWICK
My lord: we seem to be agreed.

CAUCHON rising also, but in protest.

CAUCHON
I will uphold the justice of The Church. I will strive to the utmost for this woman's salvation.

THE CHAPLAIN (*Implacably*)
I would burn her with my own hands.

Dissolve to

The ambulatory in the Cathedral at Rheims. JOAN is kneeling in prayer before one of the stations. DUNOIS comes.

Voices and footsteps echo.

DUNOIS
Come, Joan! The streets are full. They are calling for The Maid.

JOAN
No: let the King have all the glory.

DUNOIS
He only spoils the show, poor devil. Come!

JOAN shakes her head reluctantly. DUNOIS raises her.

A short interval.

JOAN
Dear Jack: I think you like me as a soldier likes his comrade.

DUNOIS
You need it, poor innocent child of God. You have not many friends at Court.

JOAN
Why do all these courtiers hate me? I have set them right. I have made Charles a real king. Then why do they not love me?

73

DUNOIS

Sim-ple-ton! Do ambitious politicians love the climbers who take the front seats from them? Why, I should be jealous of you myself if I were ambitious enough.

JOAN (*Looks at him anxiously*)
Jack, only for my voices I should lose all heart. That is why I had to steal away to pray here alone after the coronation. I'll tell you something, Jack. It is in the bells I hear my voices. Not to-day, when they all rang: that was nothing but jangling. But here in this corner where their echoes linger, or in the fields where they come from a distance through the quiet of the countryside.

The cathedral clock chimes the quarter.

JOAN
Hark!
(*She becomes rapt*)
Do you hear? "Dear child of God": but it is at the hour, when the great bell goes, it is then that St Catherine and sometimes even the blessed Michael will say things that I cannot tell beforehand. Then, oh then—

DUNOIS (*Interrupting her kindly but not sympathetically*)
Then, Joan, we shall hear whatever we fancy in the boom of the bell. I should think you were a bit cracked if I hadnt noticed that

you give me very sensible reasons for what you do, although I hear you telling others you are only obeying Madame Saint Catherine.

JOAN (*Crossly*)
Well, I have to find reasons for you, because you do not believe in my voices. But the voices come first; and I find the reasons after.

DUNOIS
Are you angry, Joan?

JOAN
Yes.
  (*Smiling*)
No: not with you. I wish you were one of the village babies.

DUNOIS
Why?

JOAN
I could nurse you for awhile.

DUNOIS
You are a bit of a woman after all.

JOAN
No: not a bit: I am a soldier and nothing else. Soldiers always nurse children when they get a chance.

DUNOIS
That is true.

He laughs.

They go to the nave. The sound of their retreating footsteps is lost in the distance.

Dissolve to

The portal.

DUNOIS opens the door; sunlight floods in. He goes out onto the steps with JOAN. A crowd outside cheers them.
"The Maid! The Maid!"

Dissolve to

The ARCHBISHOP's palace. The view is taken from a hall onto the terrace. In the garden: shrines; in the background the cathedral. It is a sunny afternoon, but a strong wind moves the trees outside. Clouds hurry across the sky.

When the scene opens CHARLES is seen hastening towards the ARCHBISHOP who is just returning from a walk in the garden.

CHARLES
Archbishop: The Maid wants to start fighting again.

The camera moves back bringing JOAN, DUNOIS, GILLES DE RAIS and LA HIRE in the hall into the picture.

THE ARCHBISHOP
Have we ceased fighting, then? Are we at peace?

CHARLES

No: but let us be content with
what we have done. Let us make
a treaty. Our luck is too good to
last.

JOAN

Luck! God has fought for us; and
you call it luck!

THE ARCHBISHOP (*Sternly*)

Maid: the King addressed himself
to me, not to you. You forget
yourself. You very often forget
yourself.

JOAN (*Unabashed, and rather
rough*)

Then speak, you: and tell him
that it is not God's will that he
should take his hands from the
plough.

THE ARCHBISHOP

If I am not so glib with the name
of God as you are, it is because I
interpret His will with the authority of The Church and of my
sacred office. When you first came
you respected it, and would not
have dared to speak as you are
now speaking.

CHARLES

Yes: she thinks she knows better
than everyone else.

JOAN

I never speak unless I know I am
right.

CHARLES
GILLES DE RAIS (*Exclaiming together*)
Just so! Ha ha!

THE ARCHBISHOP
How do you know you are right?

JOAN
My voices—

CHARLES
Oh, your voices, your voices. Why dont the voices come to me? I am King, not you.

In the adjoining room courtiers and officials, their curiosity raised by CHARLES's excited voice; they surge through the door.

JOAN
What voices do you need to tell you what the blacksmith can tell you: that you must strike while the iron is hot? I tell you we must make a dash at Compiègne and relieve it as we relieved Orleans. Then Paris will open its gates; what is your crown worth without your capital?

They all turn their heads to DUNOIS enquiringly after his opinion.

JOAN
Jack. Tell them what you think. . .

DUNOIS (*Carefully*)
I think that God was on your side: for I have not forgotten how

the wind changed, and how our
hearts changed when you came.
But I tell you as a soldier that
God is no man's daily drudge,
and no maid's either.

JOAN
But—

DUNOIS
Ah! I have not finished. . .
(*Addressing everybody*)
I know how much God did for us
through The Maid, and how
much he left me to do by my own
wits; and I tell you that your
little hour of miracles is over, and
that from this time on he who
plays the war game best will win.
But Joan goes ahead and trusts to
God: she thinks she has God in
her pocket. Up to now she has
had the numbers on her side; and
she has won. But I see that some
day she will go ahead when she
has only ten men to do the work
of a hundred. And then she will
find that God is on the side of the
big battalions. She will be taken
by the enemy. And the lucky man
that makes the capture will receive sixteen thousand pounds
from Ouarweek.

JOAN (*Flattered*)
Sixteen thousand pounds! Eh,
laddie, have they offered that for
me? There cannot be so much
money in the world.

DUNOIS

There is—in England. And now tell me, which of you will lift a finger to save Joan after she is lost in a dungeon, and the bars and bolts do not fly open at the touch of St Peter's angels: she will not be worth the life of a single soldier to us.

JOAN

Jack: you are right. I am not worth one soldier's life if God lets me be beaten; but France may think me worth my ransom after what God has done for her through me.

CHARLES

I have no money; and this coronation has cost me the last farthing I can borrow.

JOAN

I put my trust in the Church.

THE ARCHBISHOP

Woman: they will drag you through the streets, and burn you as a witch.

JOAN (*Running to him*)

Oh, my lord, I a witch! Your blessing would protect me.

THE ARCHBISHOP

I have no blessing for you while you are proud and disobedient.

JOAN

Oh, I am a poor girl. I am so ignorant that I do not know A from B. How could I be proud? And how can you say that I am disobedient when I always obey my voices, because they come from God.

THE ARCHBISHOP

The voice of God on earth is the voice of the Church Militant; and all the voices that come to you are the echoes of your own wilfulness.

JOAN

It is not true.

THE ARCHBISHOP (*Flushing angrily*)

You tell the Archbishop that he lies!

JOAN

I never said you lied. It was you that as good as said my voices lied. When have they ever lied? If you will not believe in them: even if they are only the echoes of my own commonsense, are they not always right? and are not your earthly counsels always wrong?

THE ARCHBISHOP (*Indignantly*)

It is a waste of time admonishing you. The Bastard has told you that if you persist in setting up your military conceit above the counsels of your commanders—

DUNOIS (*Interposing*)
To put it quite exactly, if you attempt to relieve the garrison in Compiègne without the same superiority in numbers you had at Orleans—

THE ARCHBISHOP (*Continuing*)
The army will disown you, and will not rescue you. And His Majesty the King has told you that the throne has not the means of ransoming you.

CHARLES
Not a penny.

THE ARCHBISHOP
You stand alone: absolutely alone.

DUNOIS
That is the truth, Joan. Heed it.

Pause.

A view of the garden over the head of JOAN. The wind bends the trees hither and thither. Ragged clouds cross the sky; only a little sun penetrates. . .

JOAN (*With great emotion*)
I thought France would have friends at the court of the King of France: and I find only wolves fighting for pieces of her torn body.

She goes from them. They stare after her in glum silence.

Fade out

The screen is dark.

The noise of battle.

Fade in

Dust clouds, horsemen . . . in flight.

JOAN, galloping into the picture.

VOICES
Back to the town!

JOAN
No, charge the enemy, for God and France.

A few of her faithfuls attempt to tear back her horse by the bridle: too late!

Burgundian soldiers charge up, surrounding JOAN.

Fights with sword and spears on all sides.

A Burgundian soldier grasps JOAN close, and tears her out of the saddle.

A *close up* of JOAN falling.

The expression of her face, an anxious question to her voices —shouts of victory from the Burgundians.

Fade out

In the courtyard at Rouen.

WARWICK, CAUCHON and two other clerics. A sunny morning.

CAUCHON
I wish your lordship good morrow.

WARWICK
Good morrow to your lordship.

CAUCHON introducing the MONK who is on his right:

CAUCHON
This, my lord, is Brother John Lemaître, of the Order of St Dominic. He is acting as deputy to the Chief Inquisitor into the evil of heresy in France. Brother John: the Earl of Warwick.

WARWICK
Your Reverence is most welcome.

The INQUISITOR smiles patiently and bows. He is a mild, elderly gentleman, but has evident reserves of authority and firmness.

CAUCHON introduces the CANON who is on his left.

CAUCHON
This gentleman is Canon John D'Estivet, of the Chapter of Bayeux. He is acting as Promoter.

WARWICK
Promoter?

CAUCHON
Prosecutor, you would call him in civil law.

WARWICK

Ah! Prosecutor. Quite, quite. I am very glad to make your acquaintance, Canon D'Estivet.

D'ESTIVET bows; he is on the young side of middle age, well mannered, but cleverer than his appearance suggests.

WARWICK

May I ask what stage the proceedings have reached? It is fully four months since I bought The Maid from the Burgundians for a very handsome sum. It is very nearly three months since I delivered her up to you, my Lord Bishop, as a person suspected of heresy.

CAUCHON

We have not been idle, my lord. We have held fifteen examinations of The Maid: six public and nine private.

THE INQUISITOR (*Always patiently smiling*)

Everything is now in order, and we proceed to trial this morning.

WARWICK (*Graciously*)

Well, that is good news, gentlemen. I will not attempt to conceal from you that our patience was becoming strained. In fact I must tell you now plainly that her death is a political necessity which I regret but cannot help. If the Church lets her go—

CAUCHON (*With fierce and menacing pride*)
If the Church lets her go, woe to the man, were he the Emperor himself, who dares lay a finger on her! The Church is not subject to political necessity, my lord.

WARWICK (*Looking hard at Cauchon*)
I should be sorry to have to act without the blessing of The Church.

CAUCHON
And yet they say Englishmen are hypocrites! You play for your side, my lord, even at the peril of your soul. I dare not go so far myself. I fear damnation.

WARWICK
If we feared anything we could never govern England, my lord.

They look hard at one another.

CAUCHON
It will be very good of your lordship to withdraw and allow the Court to assemble.

WARWICK goes.

CAUCHON, the INQUISITOR and D'ESTIVET begin to walk towards the camera which moves away from them.

A passage with a number of archers comes into view. They hurry along this passage into a large stone hall in the castle arranged for a trial at law. There are two raised chairs side by side for the BISHOP and the INQUISITOR as judges. Rows of chairs are for the canons, the doctors of law and theology, and the Dominican monks, who act as ASSESSORS.

The table is for the scribes, with stools. A heavy rough wooden stool for the prisoner. The Court is shielded from the weather by screens and curtains. Arched doors.

CAUCHON takes one of the judicial seats: and D'ESTIVET sits at the scribes' table, studying his brief.

The INQUISITOR takes the other judicial chair on CAUCHON's left.

Thirty to forty ASSESSORS hurry into the hall, among them CHAPLAIN DE STOGUMBER. Some of the ASSESSORS take their seats: others stand chatting, waiting for the proceedings to begin formally. DE STOGUMBER, aggrieved and obstinate, will not take his seat: neither will the CANON, who stands on his right.

CAUCHON (*To the Chaplain*)
Good morning, Master de Stogumber.

THE CHAPLAIN
I have to make a protest, my lord.

CAUCHON
You make a great many.

THE CHAPLAIN
Here is Master de Courcelles, Canon of Paris, who associates himself with me in my protest.

CAUCHON
Well, what is the matter?

COURCELLES (*A young priest of thirty*)
My lord: we have been at great pains to draw up an indictment of The Maid on sixty-four counts. We are now told that they have been reduced, without consulting us.

THE INQUISITOR
Master de Courcelles: I am the culprit. I am overwhelmed with admiration for the zeal displayed in your sixty-four counts: but in accusing a heretic, as in other things, enough is enough. Therefore, I have thought it well to have your sixty-four articles cut down to twelve—

COURCELLES (*Thunderstruck*)
Twelve!!!

THE INQUISITOR
Pray take your places, gentlemen; and let us proceed to business.

All who have not taken their seats, do so.

He sits down.

The INQUISITOR *drops his blandness and speaks very gravely.*

In the foreground of the picture a row of heads of the ASSESSORS, *etc. Further back, the* INQUISITOR.

THE CHAPLAIN
Well, I protest.

THE INQUISITOR
Heresy, gentlemen, heresy is the charge we have to try.

You are going to see before you a young girl, pious and chaste; for I must tell you, gentlemen, that the things said of her by our English friends are supported by no evidence, whilst there is abundant testimony that her excesses have been excesses of religion and charity and not of worldliness and wantonness. This girl is not one of those whose hard features are the sign of hard hearts and whose brazen looks and lewd demeanor condemn them before they are accused. The devilish pride that has led her into her present peril has left no mark on her countenance. It has even left no mark on her character; so that you will see a diabolical pride and a natural humility seated side by side in the selfsame soul. Therefore be on your guard! God forbid that I should tell you to harden your hearts; for her punishment, if we condemn her, will be so cruel that we should forfeit our own hope of divine mercy were there one grain of malice against her in our hearts. But if you hate cruelty—

The picture now shows the heads of ASSESSORS on the other side, and again further backwards, the INQUISITOR.

and if any man here does not hate it I command him on his soul's salvation to quit this holy court— I say, if you hate cruelty, remember that nothing is so cruel in its consequences as the toleration of heresy. Remember also that no court of law can be so cruel as the common people are to those whom they suspect of heresy. The heretic in the hands of the Holy Office is safe from violence, is assured of a fair trial, and cannot suffer death, even when guilty, if repentance follows sin. Innumerable lives of heretics have been saved because the Holy Office has taken them out of the hands of the people, and because the people have yielded them up, knowing that the Holy Office would deal with them.

Close up of the INQUISITOR.

Gentlemen, I am compassionate by nature as well as by my profession; and though the work I have

View of the entire court.

to do may seem cruel to those who do not know how much more cruel it would be to leave it undone, I would go to the stake myself sooner than do it if I did not know its necessity, its essential mercy. I ask you

to address yourselves to this trial in that conviction. Anger is a bad counsellor: cast out anger. Pity is sometimes worse: cast out pity. But do not cast out mercy. Remember only that justice comes first!

Close up of the INQUISITOR. The camera pans to CAUCHON.

Have you anything, my lord, before we proceed to trial?

CAUCHON
You have spoken for me, and spoken better than I could.

THE INQUISITOR
Let the accused be brought in.

(The trial begins.)

LADVENU *(Calling)*
The accused. Let her be brought in.

JOAN, chained by the ankles, is brought in by a guard of English soldiers. With them is the EXECUTIONER and his assistants. They lead her to the prisoner's stool, and place themselves behind it, after taking off her chain. She wears a page's black suit. Her long imprisonment and the strain of the examinations which have preceded the trial have left their mark on her; but her vitality still holds: she confronts the court unabashed, without a trace of the awe which their formal solemnity seems to require. The following trial scene may be enlivened by a succession of close ups strung together by quick dissolves and cuts.

She sits on the prisoner's stool.

THE INQUISITOR (*Kindly*)
Sit down, Joan.

You look very pale today. Are you not well?

JOAN
Thank you kindly: I am well enough. But the Bishop sent me some carp; and it made me ill.

CAUCHON
I am sorry. I told them to see that it was fresh.

JOAN
You meant to be good to me, I know; but it is a fish that does not agree with me. The English thought you were trying to poison me—

CAUCHON
THE CHAPLAIN (*Together*)
What?   No, my lord.

JOAN
The English are determined that

I shall be burnt as a witch; and
they sent their doctor to cure me;
but he was forbidden to bleed me
because the silly people believe
that a witch's witchery leaves her
if she is bled. . . Why do you
leave me in the hands of the English? I should be in the hands of
the Church. And why must I be
chained by the feet to a log of
wood? Are you afraid I will fly
away?

D'ESTIVET

Woman: it is not for you to question the court!

COURCELLES

When you were left unchained,
did you not try to escape by
jumping from a tower sixty feet
high? If you cannot fly like a
witch, how is it that you are still
alive?

JOAN

I suppose because the tower was
not so high then. It has grown
higher every day since you began
asking me questions about it.

D'ESTIVET

Why did you jump from the
tower?

JOAN

Why would anybody leave a prison if they could get out?

93

D'ESTIVET
You tried to escape?

JOAN
Of course I did.

D'ESTIVET (*Rising*)
That is a confession of heresy. I call the attention of the court to it.

JOAN
Heresy, he calls it! Am I a heretic because I try to escape from prison?

D'ESTIVET
If you are in the hands of the Church, and you wilfully take yourself out of its hands, you are deserting the Church; and that is heresy.

JOAN
It is great nonsense. Nobody could be such a fool as to think that.

D'ESTIVET
You hear, my lord, how I am reviled in the execution of my duty by this woman.

He sits down indignantly.

CAUCHON
I have warned you before, Joan, that you are doing yourself no good by these curt answers.

JOAN

But you will not talk sense to me.
I am reasonable if you will be
reasonable.

THE INQUISITOR (*Interposing*)

This is not yet in order. You forget, Master Promoter, that the
proceedings have not been formally opened. The time for questions is after she has sworn on the
Gospels to tell us the whole truth.

JOAN

I have said again and again that I
will tell you all that concerns this
trial but I cannot tell you the
whole truth: God does not allow
the whole truth to be told. You
do not understand it when I tell
it. I am weary of this argument:
we have been over it nine times
already. I have sworn as much as
I will swear; and I will swear no
more.

COURCELLES

My lord: she should be put to the
torture.

THE INQUISITOR

You hear, Joan? That is what
happens to the obdurate. Has she
been shown the instruments?

THE EXECUTIONER

They are ready, my lord. She has
seen them.

JOAN

If you tear me limb from limb until you separate my soul from my body you will get nothing out of me beyond what I have told you. Besides, I cannot bear to be hurt; and if you hurt me I will say anything you like. But I will take it all back afterwards; so what is the use of it?

LADVENU

There is much in that. We should proceed mercifully.

COURCELLES

But the torture is customary.

THE INQUISITOR

If the accused will confess voluntarily then its use cannot be justified.

COURCELLES

But she refuses to take the oath.

LADVENU (*Disgusted*)

Do you want to torture the girl for the mere pleasure of it?

COURCELLES (*Bewildered*)

But it is not a pleasure. It is the law. It is always done.

CAUCHON (*Decisively*)

It will not be done today if it is not necessary.

COURCELLES
Your lordship is merciful, of course, but it is a great responsibility to depart from the usual practice.

JOAN
Thou art a rare noodle, Master. Do what was done last time be thy rule, eh?

COURCELLES (*Rising*)
Thou wanton: dost thou dare call me noodle?

THE INQUISITOR
Patience, Master, patience: I fear you will soon be only too terribly avenged.

COURCELLES (*Mutters*)
Noodle indeed!

He sits down, much discontented.

THE INQUISITOR
Meanwhile, let us not be moved by the rough side of a shepherd lass's tongue.

JOAN
Nay; I am no shepherd lass.

THE INQUISITOR
This is not a time for vanity, Joan. You stand in great peril.

JOAN
I know it: have I not been punished for my vanity? If I had

97

not worn my cloth of gold surcoat in battle like a fool, that Burgundian soldier would never have pulled me off my horse; and I should not have been here.

CAUCHON
Come! We are wasting time on trifles. Joan: I am going to put a most solemn question to you. Take care how you answer; for your life and salvation are at stake on it. Will you for all you have said and done, accept the judgment of God's Church on earth? Will you submit your case to the Church?

JOAN
I am a faithful child of the Church. I will obey the Church—

CAUCHON (Hopefully leaning forward)
You will?

JOAN
—provided it does not demand anything impossible.

CAUCHON sinks back in his chair with a heavy sigh.

D'ESTIVET
She imputes to the Church the error and folly of commanding the impossible.

JOAN
If you command me to declare that all the visions and revela-

tions I have had, were not from God, then that is impossible: I will not decare it for anything in the world. And in case the Church should bid me do anything contrary to the command I have from God, I will not consent to it, no matter what it may be.

THE ASSESSORS (*Sharp and indignant*)
Oh! The Church contrary to God! Flat heresy. This is beyond everything!

D'ESTIVET (*Throwing down his brief*)
My lord: do you need anything more than this?

CAUCHON
Woman: you have said enough to burn ten heretics. Will you not be warned? Will you not understand?

THE INQUISITOR
If the Church Militant tells you that your revelations and visions are sent by the devil to tempt you to your damnation, will you not believe that the Church is wiser than you?

JOAN
I believe that God is wiser than I; all the things that you call my

crimes have come to me by the command of God. I say that I have done them by the order of God. If any Churchman says to the contrary I shall not mind him.

LADVENU (*Pleading with her urgently*)
You do not know what you are saying, child. Do you want to kill yourself? Listen. Do you not believe that you are subject to the Church of God on earth?

JOAN
Yes. When have I ever denied it?

LADVENU
Good. That means, does it not, that you are subject to our Lord the Pope, to the Cardinals, the Archbishops, and the bishops for whom his lordship stands here today?

JOAN
God must be served first.

D'ESTIVET
Then your voices command you not to submit yourself to the Church Militant?

JOAN
My voices do not tell me to disobey the Church; but God must be served first.

CAUCHON

And you, and not the Church, are to be the judge?

JOAN

What other judgment can I judge by than my own?

THE ASSESSORS (*Scandalized*)

Oh!

They cannot find words.

CAUCHON

Dare you pretend, after what you have said, that you are in a state of grace?

JOAN

If I am not, may God bring me to it; if I am, may God keep me in it!

LADVENU

That is a very good reply, my lord.

D'ESTIVET

With all due respect I must emphasize the gravity of two blasphemous crimes: first, she wears men's clothes, which is indecent, unnatural and abominable. Second, she has intercourse with evil spirits.

JOAN

Is the blessed St Catherine an evil spirit? Is St Margaret? Is Michael the Archangel?

101

COURCELLES

How do you know that the spirit which appears to you is an Archangel? Does he not appear to you as a naked man?

JOAN

Do you think God cannot afford clothes for him?

The ASSESSORS cannot help smiling, especially as the joke is against COURCELLES.

THE INQUISITOR

For the last time, will you put off that impudent attire, and dress as becomes your sex?

JOAN

I will not.

D'ESTIVET (*Pouncing*)

The sin of disobedience, my lord.

JOAN (*Distressed*)

But my voices tell me I must dress as a soldier.

LADVENU

Joan, Joan: does not that prove to you that the voices are the voices of evil spirits? Can you suggest to us one good reason why an angel of God should give you such shameless advice?

JOAN

Why, yes: what can be plainer commonsense? I was a soldier living among soldiers. If I were to dress as a woman they would think of me as a woman; if I dress as a soldier they think of me as a soldier, and I can live with them as I do at home with my brothers. That is why St Catherine tells me I must not dress as a woman until she gives me leave.

COURCELLES

When will she give you leave?

JOAN

When you take me out of the hands of the English soldiers. Do you want me to live with them in petticoats?

LADVENU

My lord: what she says is, God knows, very wrong and shocking; but there is a grain of worldly sense in it such as might impose on a simple village maiden.

JOAN

If we were as simple in the village as you are in your courts and palaces, there would soon be no wheat to make bread for you.

CAUCHON

That is the thanks you get for trying to save her, Brother Martin.

LADVENU

Joan: we are all trying to save you. His lordship is trying to save you. The Inquisitor could not be more just to you if you were his own daughter. But you are blinded by a terrible pride and self-sufficiency.

JOAN

Why do you say that? I have said nothing wrong. I cannot understand.

THE INQUISITOR

The blessed Saint Athanasius has laid it down in his creed that those who cannot understand are damned. The simplicity of a darkened mind is no better than the simplicity of a beast.

JOAN

There is great wisdom in the simplicity of a beast, let me tell you; and sometimes great foolishness in the wisdom of scholars.

LADVENU

Joan: do you see that man who stands behind you?

He indicates the EXECUTIONER.

JOAN turns and looks at the man.

JOAN

Your torturer? But the Bishop said I was not to be tortured.

LADVENU

That man is not only the torturer: he is also the Executioner.

(*Calling on the Executioner*)
Are you prepared for the burning
of a heretic this day?

THE EXECUTIONER

Yes, Master.

LADVENU

Is the stake ready?

THE EXECUTIONER

It is. In the market-place. The
English have built it too high for
me to get near her and make the
death easier.

JOAN (*Horrified*)

But you are not going to burn me
now?

THE INQUISITOR

You realize it at last.

LADVENU

There are eight hundred English
soldiers waiting to take you to the
market-place the moment the
sentence of excommunication has
passed the lips of your judges.

JOAN (*Looking round desper-
ately for rescue*)

Oh God!

LADVENU

Do not despair, Joan. The Church
is merciful. You can save yourself.

JOAN (*Hopefully*)
Yes: my voices promised me I should not be burnt. St Catherine bade me be bold.

CAUCHON
Woman: are you quite mad? Do you not yet see that your voices have deceived you?

JOAN
Oh no: that is impossible.

LADVENU (*Pressing the point hard*)
Have your voices kept a single promise to you since you were taken at Compiègne? The devil has betrayed you. The Church holds out its arms to you.

JOAN (*Despairing*)
Oh, it is true: it is true: my voices have deceived me. I have been mocked by devils. I have dared and dared; but only a fool will walk into a fire: God, who gave me my commonsense, cannot will me to do that.

LADVENU
Now God be praised that He has saved you at the eleventh hour!

He hurries to the vacant seat at the scribes' table and snatches a sheet of paper on which he sets to work writing eagerly.

CAUCHON
Amen!

JOAN

What must I do?

CAUCHON

You must sign a solemn recantation of your heresy.

JOAN

Sign? I cannot write.

CAUCHON

You have signed many letters before.

JOAN

Yes; but someone held my hand and guided the pen. I can make my mark.

The CHAPLAIN who has been listening with growing alarm:

THE CHAPLAIN

My lord: do you mean that you are going to allow this woman to escape us?

THE INQUISITOR

Master de Stogumber, you know the law.

The CHAPLAIN rising purple with fury:

THE CHAPLAIN

I know what the Earl of Warwick will do when he hears of it. There are eight hundred men at the gate who will see that this abominable witch is burnt in spite of your teeth.

THE ASSESSORS (*Meanwhile*)
What is this? This is an intolerable fellow. He must be mad or drunk.

The INQUISITOR rising:

THE INQUISITOR
Silence, pray! Gentlemen: pray silence! Master Chaplain: bethink you of your holy office: I direct you to sit down.

The CHAPLAIN, folding his arms doggedly, his face working convulsively:

THE CHAPLAIN
I will N O T sit down.

The INQUISITOR placidly resuming his seat:

THE INQUISITOR
If you will not sit, you must stand: that is all.

THE CHAPLAIN
I will N O T stand.

He flings himself back into his chair.

LADVENU rising with the paper in his hand:

LADVENU
My lord: here is the form of recantation for The Maid to sign.

CAUCHON
Read it to her.

JOAN
Do not trouble. I will sign it.

THE INQUISITOR
You must know what you are putting your hand to.

LADVENU *(Reading quietly)*
"I, Joan, commonly called The
Maid, a miserable sinner, do confess that I have most grievously
sinned in the following articles: I
have pretended to have revelations from God and the angels
and the blessed saints, and per-
versely rejected the Church's
warning that these were tempta-
tions by demons. I have blas-
phemed abominably by wearing
an immodest dress, contrary to
the Holy Scripture and the canons
of the Church. Also I have
clipped my hair in the style of
a man. I have incited men to slay
each other, invoking evil spirits
to delude them, and stubbornly
and most blasphemously im-
puting these sins to Almighty
God. All of which sins I now re-
nounce and abjure and I will
never return to my errors, but
will remain in communion with
our Holy Church and in obedi-
ence to our Holy Father the Pope
at Rome. All this I swear by God
Almighty and the Holy Gospels.
In witness whereto I sign my
name to this recantation."

THE INQUISITOR
You understand this, Joan?

JOAN *(Listless)*
It is plain enough, sir.

THE INQUISITOR
And it is true?

JOAN
It may be true. If it were not true, the fire would not be ready for me in the market-place.

LADVENU takes up his pen and a book, and goes quickly to JOAN lest she should compromise herself again.

LADVENU
Come, child: let me guide your hand. Take the pen.

She does so; and they begin to write, using the book as a desk.

J.E.H.A.N.E. So. Now make your mark by yourself.

JOAN makes her mark and gives him back the pen, tormented by the rebellion of her soul against her mind and body.

JOAN
There!

LADVENU replaces the pen on the table and hands the recantation to CAUCHON with a reverence.

LADVENU
Praise be to God, my brothers, the lamb has returned to the flock; and the shepherd rejoices in her more than in ninety and nine just persons.

He returns to his seat.

The INQUISITOR takes the paper from CAUCHON.

THE INQUISITOR
We declare thee by this act set free from the danger of excommunication in which thou stoodest.

He throws the paper down to the table.

But that thou mayst repent thy errors in solitary contemplation, and be shielded from all temptation to return to them, we, for the good of thy soul and for a penance, do condemn thee to eat the bread of sorrow and drink the water of affliction to the end of thy earthly days in perpetual imprisonment.

JOAN rising in terrible anger:

JOAN
Perpetual imprisonment! Am I not then to be set free?

LADVENU (*Mildly shocked*)
Set free, child, after such wickedness as yours! What are you dreaming of?

JOAN
Give me that writing.

She rushes to the table; snatches up the paper; and tears it into fragments.

Light your fire: do you think I dread it as much as the life of a rat in a hole? My voices were right.

LADVENU
Joan! Joan!

111

The word gives great offence.

Indignant exclamations.

JOAN
Yes: they told me you were fools.

You promised me my life; but you lied.

You think that life is nothing but not being stone dead. I could do without my war horse; I could drag about in a skirt; I could let the banners and the trumpets and the knights and soldiers pass me and leave me behind as they leave the other women, if only I could still hear the wind in the trees, the larks in the sunshine, and the blessed, blessed church bells that send my angel voices floating to me on the wind. But without these things I cannot live; and by your wanting to take them away from me, or from any human creature, I know that your counsel is of the devil, and that mine is of God.

THE ASSESSORS (*In great commotion*)
Blasphemy! Blasphemy! She is possessed. The devil is in our midst.

D'ESTIVET (*Shouting above the din*)
She is a relapsed heretic. I call for her excommunication.

THE CHAPLAIN (*To the Executioner*)

Light your fire, man. To the stake with her.

The EXECUTIONER and his assistants hurry out through the courtyard.

LADVENU

You wicked girl: if your counsel were of God would He not deliver you?

JOAN

His ways are not your ways. He wills that I go through the fire to His bosom; for I am His child, and you are not fit that I should live among you. That is my last word for you.

Soldiers seize her.

CAUCHON (*Rising*)

Not yet.

They wait. CAUCHON turns to the INQUISITOR with an enquiring look. The INQUISITOR nods affirmatively, also rising. They intone the sentence antiphonally.

CAUCHON

We decree that thou art a relapsed heretic.

THE INQUISITOR

Cast out from the unity of the Church.

CAUCHON

Sundered from her body.

113

THE INQUISITOR

We declare that thou must be excommunicate.

CAUCHON

And now abandon thee to the secular power.

The INQUISITOR resumes his seat.

CAUCHON

And if any true sign of penitence appear in thee, to permit our Brother Martin to administer to thee the sacrament of penance.

THE CHAPLAIN

Into the fire with the witch!

He rushes at JOAN, and helps the soldiers to push her out.

The ASSESSORS rise in disorder. Excited exclamations and shouts.

CAUCHON

This is irregular. The representative of the secular arm should be here to receive her from us.

THE INQUISITOR

That man is an incorrigible fool.

CAUCHON

Brother Martin; see that everything is done in order.

LADVENU

My place is at her side, my lord. You must exercise your own authority.

He hurries out.

(Photograph by Foto-Bureau, Wouter van Heusden)

THE NETHERLANDS (Toneelgroep Theater, Arnheim, 1966; directed by Theo Kling; designed by Roger Chailloux) . *Scene iv.* Seated left: Hans Tiemeijer as Cauchon; seated right: Hans Croiset as Warwick; right of Warwick: Bernhard Droog as De Stogumber.

AUSTRALIA (Australian Elizabethan Theatre Trust in association with Adelaide University Theatre Guild, Adelaide, 1962; directed by Norman D. Philbrick). *Scene v.* Zoe Caldwell as Joan; Ron Haddrick as Dunois; Roger McDougall as the Dauphin.

ENGLAND (London, 1924; directed by Bernard Shaw and Lewis Casson;
designed by Charles Ricketts). *Scene v.* Sybil Thorndike as Joan; left
of Joan: Raymond Massey as La Hire; Robert Horton as Dunois; right
of Joan: Ernest Thesiger as the Dauphin; Milton Rosmer as Gilles
de Rais; Robert Cunningham as the Archbishop.

RUSSIA (Moscow Theatre in Honor of Lenin Youth League, Moscow, 1958; directed by A. P. Petrochenko, based on original production by B. C. Kantsel). *Scene vi.* E. A. Fadeyeva as Joan.

SWEDEN (Vasa Theatre, Stockholm, 1964; directed by Per Gerhard). *Scene v.* Maj-Britt Nilsson as Joan; left of Joan: Sven Wollter as Dunois; right of Joan: Heinz Hopf as the Dauphin.

(Photograph by Beata Bergstro

THE NETHERLANDS (Netherlands Comedy, Amsterdam, 1954; directed by Douglas Seale). *Scene vi*. Ellen Vogel as Joan.

(Photograph by Foto-Bureau, Wouter van Heusden)

FRANCE (Théâtre des Arts, Paris, 1925; directed by Georges Pitoëff). *Scene vi*. Ludmilla Pitoëff as Joan.

THE NETHERLANDS (Toneelgroep Theater, Arnheim, 1966; directed by Theo Kling; designed by Roger Chailloux). *Scene vi*. Henry Orri as Joan; extreme left: Hans Tiemeijer as Cauchon.

GERMANY (Deutsches Theater, Berlin, 1934; directed by Heinz Hilpert). *Scene vi*. Paula Wessely as Joan.

UNITED STATES (Tyrone Guthrie Theatre, Minneapolis, Minnesota, 1964; directed by Douglas Campbell). *Epilogue*. Ellen Geer as Joan; left of Joan: George Grizzard as the Dauphin; right: Lee Richardson as Cauchon.

Fade out

The screen is dark. The sound of Church bells from near and afar, high pitched, booming, and clashing peals clang together for several seconds. Then:

Gradual fade in (the bells continue)

A chattering mob of sightseers crowding the steps of a church in a street between the Palace and the market-place: [5]

Chattering.

A British MAN-AT-ARMS, off duty, is out to see the fun. He is not on the steps but in the foreground.

Noise of the approaching show heard.

All become silent on hearing the noise of the approaching show, and turn in that direction.

Some are eager and curious, some are gaping stupidly, a few picked faces register pity or horror.

A squad of mounted soldiers forces a way through the crowd. Following them, a body of men-at-arms marching in ordered files.

---

[5] In an earlier draft, the scene began with the camera exploring the stake. See Appendix G.

Then JOAN, in a white shift, hurried along by three or four soldiers.

DE STOGUMBER is close on her heels, pushing her savagely as she hangs back, piteously begging for a cross.

LADVENU is with him, full of pity, but useless.

JOAN is trying to stop; but the men-at-arms drag, and DE STOGUMBER pushes, not continuously but with violent gestures.

JOAN
A cross. I want a cross. There is one in the church. You have no right to keep my Savior from me.

DE STOGUMBER
Witch. Sorceress. Strike her on her blaspheming mouth. To the fire with her.

LADVENU (*Remonstrating*)
Brother, brother—

JOAN (*As she is dragged away*)
Oh, is there no child of Christ here who will give me a blessed cross—

She is pushed so violently that she falls. A soldier drags her up again.

SOLDIER
Come on, will you.

DE STOGUMBER, kicking her, says:

116

DE STOGUMBER

On, strumpet. On, sorceress. To
the fire. To the fire.

She is whirled away.

Further ordered files bring up
the rear.

The crowd closes in behind
them and follows.

LADVENU remains, heartbroken,
waiting for the crowd to clear
off the church steps.

The MAN-AT-ARMS, who is
troubled with a lively desire to
kick DE STOGUMBER, also remains.

Among the stragglers are several porters with bundles of
faggots on their shoulders.
Some of them are women.

LADVENU, the steps being now
clear, rushes into the church.

The MAN-AT-ARMS suddenly
pounces on the last straggling
porter, an old woman; tears
the bundle from her shoulders
and takes a stick out of it; lifts
the bundle and thumps it on
her shoulders again; gives her
a coin.

OLD WOMAN

God save your honor. Long live
the goddams!

She hobbles off.

The MAN-AT-ARMS sets the stick leaning against the lowest church step, and strikes it in the middle with his foot, breaking it in two.

He picks up the pieces; sits down on the steps; takes an old bowstring out of his pouch, and ties the two pieces of stick into the form of a cross.

LADVENU hurries out of the church carrying a processional cross—a gold cross on a long black staff.

MAN-AT-ARMS

Thats no use, father. She cant take that into the fire with her. I bet she prefers this. Here!

Consecrate it for her.

(Holding out the sticks)

LADVENU, touching the cross, says:

LADVENU

In the name of the Father, the Son and the Holy Ghost, Amen. And for this be all your sins forgiven to you.

He rushes off after the procession.

The MAN-AT-ARMS runs after him.

Long shot.

The market-place, Rouen; many men-at-arms.

118

Crowd, the stake.

Close up of the stake and platform.

JOAN is clasped to the stake by
the iron waist-band; but she is
not otherwise bound.

LADVENU is holding the cross
before her. She is praying to
it intensely.

Wisps of smoke are curling
round the platform.

The EXECUTIONER comes up the
ladder.

EXECUTIONER, seizing LADVENU
and drawing him to the ladder,
says:

THE EXECUTIONER
Now, father. Down quickly. The
fires I make are not to be trifled
with.

JOAN
Oh yes, father, go. Go quickly;
and God bless you for ever and
ever.

THE EXECUTIONER
Quick, before the oil catches.

He drags LADVENU down the
ladder.

JOAN is left alone without the
cross.

An expression of anguish comes on her face.

VOICE OF MAN-AT-ARMS
High, Judy, look! Catch!

JOAN's face lights up as she looks. She stretches out her arms hungrily for the cross of two sticks. It flies up from below. She catches it and hugs it to her breast.

There is a moment of terrible expectation.

Then the oil catches and a great wall of flame shoots up and hides her.

JOAN (*In the fire*)
Jesus! Jesus! Jesus!

Fade in

The room in the castle with the judicial chains, etc.

Nobody is present; the evening sun casts long and narrow shadows. From the back, WAR-WICK's voice:

WARWICK
Hallo.

Silence.

Hallo, there!

Silence.

WARWICK appears in the background under the arch.

Hallo!

Silence.

The silence is broken by someone frantically howling and sobbing.

What in the devil's name—?

The CHAPLAIN staggers in from the back, passing WARWICK, his face streaming with tears. He stumbles to the prisoner's stool, and throws himself upon it with heart-rending sobs.

He goes to him.

WARWICK
What is it, Master John?

THE CHAPLAIN (*Clutching at his hands*)
My lord, my lord: for Christ's sake pray for my wretched guilty soul.

WARWICK (*Soothing him*)
Yes, yes.

THE CHAPLAIN (*Blubbering miserably*)
I did not know what it would be like; when you see the thing you have done; when it is blinding your eyes, stifling your nostrils, tearing your heart, then—then—

Falling on his knees.

Oh, God, take away the sight from me! Oh Christ, deliver me from this fire that is consuming me! She cried to Thee in the midst of it. She is in Thy bosom; and I am in hell for evermore.

WARWICK

Summarily pulling him to his feet.

Come, come, man! You must pull yourself together. We shall have the whole town talking of this.

121

He throws him not too gently into a chair.

If you have not the nerve to see these things, why do you **not do** as I do, and stay away?

THE CHAPLAIN (*Bewildered and submissive*)
She asked for a cross. A soldier gave her two sticks tied together. Thank God he was an Englishman!

WARWICK
Hush! Someone is coming.

LADVENU appears in the archway. He carries a bishop's cross: he is very grave and composed.

I am informed that it is all over, Brother Martin.

LADVENU (*Enigmatically*)
We do not know, my lord. It may have only just begun.

WARWICK
What does that mean, exactly?

LADVENU
I took this cross from the Church for her that she might see it to the last. When the fire crept round us, and she saw that if I held the cross before her I should be burnt myself, she warned me to get down and save myself. My lord: a girl

who could think of another's danger in such a moment was not inspired by the devil. When I had to snatch the cross from her sight, she looked up to heaven. And I do not believe that the heavens were empty. I firmly believe that the Savior appeared to her then in His tenderest glory. She called to Him and died. This is not the end for her, but the beginning.

Silence.

The distant bell continues to ring.

Rising frantically, he shrieks:

THE CHAPLAIN

I will go pray among her ashes. I am no better than Judas! I will hang myself.

WARWICK

Quick, Brother Martin: follow him: he will do himself some mischief.

LADVENU hurries out.

WARWICK alone. He walks towards the camera, with the expression of an undefined sentiment. From the side, a door is heard opening, and somebody enters. WARWICK looks up—it is the EXECUTIONER.

THE EXECUTIONER

I am come to tell your lordship that your orders have been obeyed.

123

He nods, wrapt in thought. Suddenly he remarks:

WARWICK

Master Executioner: I have your word, have I, that nothing remains, not a bone, not a nail, not a hair.

THE EXECUTIONER

Her heart would not burn, my lord. But everything that was left is at the bottom of the river. You have heard the last of her.

WARWICK (*With a wry smile, thinking of what Ladvenu said*) The last of her? Hm! I wonder!

WARWICK says these words in a significant *close up,* which slowly

Dissolves [6]

To the title

EPILOGUE

Superimposed over this title appears the sub-title

A NIGHT IN JUNE 1456

The title gradually

Dissolves

[6] Shaw contemplated omitting the play's Epilogue entirely, substituting a visual ending. Two different versions of the alternate endings are in the papers at the British Museum. See Appendix H for the shorter version, Appendix I for the longer. The film's Epilogue, it should be noted, is considerably shorter than the play's Epilogue.

to a wide terrace window.

The outlines of a park can be distinguished in the darkness outside.

Distant thunder; flashes of lightning on the horizon. The *camera moves* back into the room, revealing CHARLES lying in bed. The bed is raised on a dais of two steps; its canopy bears the Royal Arms in embroidery. Except for the canopy and the huge down pillows there is nothing to distinguish it from a broad settee with bed clothes and a valance.

CHARLES is asleep. On his left is a little table with a picture of the Virgin, lighted by candles. A distant clock strikes the half-hour softly. An open book lies on the bed; it contains pictures of Fouquet's Boccaccio.

The *camera pans* and again brings the wide terrace window in the background into the picture. It is a very high window. Flashes of lightning, distant thunder.

Suddenly—a gust of wind throws open the casements. The candles flicker. For several moments, bright flashes of lightning, illuminating a figure standing on the threshold.

CHARLES (*Crying out in his sleep*)
Who is there? Help! Murder!

JOAN

Easy, Charlie, easy. No one can hear thee. Thou art asleep.

She is dimly seen in a pallid light by the bedside. The window is still open; the wind sweeping through the trees outside makes a rushing sound in the leaves.

Peeping from underneath the bedclothes.

CHARLES

Joan! Are you a ghost, Joan?

The light grows brighter; she is plainly visible. He sits up.

JOAN

I am but a dream that thourt dreaming. Thou looks older, lad,

CHARLES
Am I really asleep?

JOAN
Fallen asleep over thy silly book.

CHARLES
Are you really dead?

JOAN
As dead as anybody ever is, laddie. I am out of the body.

CHARLES
Did it hurt much?

JOAN
Did what hurt much?

CHARLES
Being burnt.

JOAN

Oh, that! I cannot remember very
well. I think it did at first; but
then it all got mixed up; and I
was not in my right mind. How
hast been ever since?

CHARLES

Oh, not so bad. Do you know, I
actually lead my army out and
win battles?

JOAN

No! Did I make a man of thee
after all, Charlie? Now tell me
what has happened since you wise
men knew no better than to make
a heap of cinders of me.

CHARLES

Your case was tried over again.
And the courts have declared that
the sentence on you is broken,
annihilated, annulled: null, non-
existent, without value or effect.

JOAN

I was burned, all the same. Can
they unburn me?

CHARLES

If they could, they would think
twice before they did it. But I
think you might say a word of
thanks to me for having had justice done at last.

CAUCHON

Appears at the window be-
tween them.

Liar!

CHARLES
Thank you!

JOAN
Why, if it isnt Peter Cauchon!

CAUCHON
I arraign the justice of Man. It is not the justice of God.

JOAN
Still dreaming of justice, Peter? See what justice came to with me! But what has happened to thee? Art dead or alive?

CAUCHON
Dead. Dishonored. They pursued me beyond the grave. They excommunicated my dead body; they dug it up and flung it into the common sewer. Yet God is my witness I was just: I was merciful; I was faithful to my light; I could do no other than I did.

CHARLES

Scrambling out of the sheets and enthroning himself on the side of the bed.

You people with your heads in the sky spend all your time trying to turn the world upside down; but I take the world as it is, and see that top-side-up is right-side-up; and I keep my nose pretty close to the ground.

JOAN
Be the English gone?

Coming through the darkness on JOAN's left. The candles illuminate his armor and surcoat cheerfully.

DUNOIS

The English are gone.

JOAN
Praised be God! Jack: wert thou God's captain to the death?

DUNOIS
I am not dead. My body is very comfortably asleep in my bed at Chateaudun; but my spirit is called here by yours. I give you best, lassie. I wrote a fine letter to set you right at the new trial. Perhaps I should never have let the priests burn you; but I was busy fighting; and it was the Church's business, not mine. There was no use in both of us being burned, was there?

A long gentle knocking is heard.

CHARLES
Come in.

The door opens; and an old priest, white-haired, bent, with a silly but benevolent smile, comes in and trots over to JOAN.

NEWCOMER
Excuse me, gentle lords and ladies. Do not let me disturb you. Only a poor old harmless English rector, formerly chaplain to the cardinal: to my lord of Winchester.

He looks at them enquiringly.

Did you say anything? I am a little deaf, unfortunately. Also a little—well, not always in my right mind, perhaps.

JOAN
Poor old John! What brought thee to this state?

DE STOGUMBER
I tell my folks they must be very careful. I say to them, "If you only saw what you think about you would think quite differently about it. It would give you a great shock." And they all say "Yes, parson; we all know you are a kind man, and would not harm a fly." That is a great comfort to me, for once I did a very cruel thing, because I did not know what cruelty was like. I had not seen it, you know. That is the great thing: you must see it. And then you are redeemed and saved.

JOAN
Well, if I saved all those he would have been cruel to if he had not been cruel to me, I was not burnt for nothing, was I?

DE STOGUMBER
Oh no; it was not you. My sight is bad; I cannot distinguish your features: but you are not she: oh no: she was burned to a cinder: dead and gone.

THE EXECUTIONER

Stepping from behind the bed curtains on CHARLES's right, the bed being between them.

She is more alive than you, old man. I was a master at my craft: better than the master of Paris; but I could not kill The Maid. She is up and alive everywhere.

WARWICK

Sallying from the bed curtains on the other side and coming to JOAN's left hand.

Madam: my congratulations on your rehabilitation. I feel that I owe you an apology.

JOAN
Oh, please dont mention it.

WARWICK (*Pleasantly*)
The burning was purely political.

JOAN
I bear no malice, my lord.

WARWICK
Just so. Very kind of you to meet me in that way. The truth is, these political necessities sometimes turn out to be political mistakes; and this one was a veritable howler; for your spirit conquered us, madam, in spite of our fagots.

A clerical-looking gentleman in black frockcoat and trousers, and tall hat, in the fashion of the year 1920, suddenly appears before them in the corner on their right. They all stare at him. Then they burst into uncontrollable laughter.

GENTLEMAN
Why this mirth, gentlemen?

WARWICK
I congratulate you on having invented a most extraordinarily comic dress.

GENTLEMAN
I do not understand. You are all in fancy dress; I am properly dressed.

DUNOIS
All dress is fancy dress, is it not, except our natural skins?

GENTLEMAN
Pardon me; I am here on serious business, and cannot engage in frivolous discussions.

He takes out a paper, and assumes a dry, official manner.

I am sent to announce to you that Joan of Arc, formerly known as The Maid, having been the subject of an inquiry instituted by the Bishop of Orleans—

JOAN

Interrupting.

Ah! They remember me still in Orleans.

GENTLEMAN

Emphatically, to mark his indignation at the interruption.

—by the Bishop of Orleans, into the claim of the said Joan of Arc to be canonized as a saint—

JOAN

Again interrupting.

But I never made any such claim.

GENTLEMAN

As before.

—the Church has examined the claim exhaustively in the usual course, and, having admitted the said Joan successively to the ranks of Venerable and Blessed—

JOAN

Chuckling.

Me venerable!

GENTLEMAN

—has finally declared her to have been endowed with heroic virtues and favored with private revelations, and calls the said Venerable and Blessed Joan to the Communion of the Church Triumphant as Saint Joan.

JOAN

Rapt.

Saint Joan!

GENTLEMAN

On every 30th day of May, being the anniversary of the death of the said most blessed daughter of God, there shall in every Catholic church to the end of time be celebrated the special office in commemoration of her; and it shall be lawful to dedicate a special chapel to her, and to place her image on its altar in every such church. And it shall be lawful and laudable for the faithful to kneel and address their prayers through her to the Mercy Seat.

133

She falls on her knees, still rapt.

Putting up his paper and retiring beside the EXECUTIONER.

Raising JOAN.

The ARCHBISHOP and the IN-QUISITOR are now seen on the right and kneeling to her, left of CAUCHON.

Kneeling to her.

Kneeling to her.

JOAN
Oh no. It is for the saint to kneel.

GENTLEMAN

In Basilica Vaticana, the sixteenth day of May, nineteen hundred and twenty.

DUNOIS

Half an hour to burn you, dear Saint: and four centuries to find out the truth about you.

CAUCHON
The girls in the field praise thee; for thou hast raised their eyes; and they see that there is nothing between them and heaven.

DUNOIS

The dying soldiers praise thee, because thourt a shield of glory between them and the judgment.

THE ARCHBISHOP

The princes of the Church praise thee, because thou hast redeemed the faith.

WARWICK

Kneeling to her.

The cunning counsellors praise thee, because thou hast cut the knots in which they have tied their own souls.

DE STOGUMBER

Kneeling to her.

The foolish old men on their death beds praise thee, because their sins against thee are turned into blessings.

THE INQUISITOR

Kneeling to her.

The judges in the blindness and bondage of the law praise thee, because thou hast vindicated the vision and the freedom of the living soul.

THE EXECUTIONER

Kneeling to her.

The tormentors and executioners praise thee, because thou hast shewn that their hands are guiltless of the death of the soul.

CHARLES

Kneeling to her.

The unpretending praise thee, because thou hast taken upon thyself the heroic burdens that are too heavy for them.

JOAN

Woe unto me when all men praise me! I bid you remember that I

A gust of wind—the candles are extinguished. Darkness blots out the room.

The voices exclaim in dark irregular chorus.

In the darkness they are heard discreetly stealing away.

Gradually the screen lights up again; the rays of the moon reveal outlines. CHARLES and JOAN alone have stayed behind.

Seated on the bed, yawning.

He does so.

Sadly.

Mumbling in his pillows.

He sleeps. Darkness envelops the bed. The first stroke of midnight is heard softly from a distant bell. The last remain-

am a saint, and that saints can work miracles. And now tell me: shall I rise from the dead, and come back to you a living woman?

JOAN'S VOICE
What! Must I burn again? Are none of you ready to receive me?

DUNOIS
Forgive us, Joan: we are not yet good enough for you.

CHARLES

Poor old Joan! They have all run away from you; and what can I do but go back to bed too?

JOAN

Good night, Charlie.

CHARLES

Goo ni.

ing rays of light gather into a white radiance descending on JOAN. The hour continues to strike.

From afar the voices of a choir, accompanied by organ and orchestral music.

Dissolve

JOAN

O God that madest this beautiful earth, when will it be ready to receive Thy saints? How long, O Lord, how long?

THE END

APPENDIXES

Appendix A MOTION PICTURES WITH SCREENPLAYS BY BERNARD SHAW
(date is year of release)

Cathedral Scene from *Saint Joan* (1927)
Screenplay: Bernard Shaw
Director: Widgery Newman
Producer: Vivian Van Dam (Phonofilms)
Star: Sybil Thorndike as Joan

How He Lied to Her Husband (1931)
Screenplay: Bernard Shaw
Director: Cecil Lewis
Producer: John Maxwell (British International Pictures)
Stars: Robert Harris, Vera Lennox, and Edmund Gwenn as He, She, and Her Husband

Arms and the Man (1932)
Screenplay: Bernard Shaw
Director: Cecil Lewis
Producer: John Maxwell (British International Pictures)
Stars: Barry Jones as Bluntschli, Anne Grey as Raina, Maurice Colebourne as Sergius, Angela Baddeley as Louka, Frederick Lloyd as Petkoff, Margaret Scudamore as Catherine

Pygmalion (1938)
Screenplay: Bernard Shaw (adaptation by Cecil Lewis, W. P. Lipscomb, and Ian Dalrymple)
Directors: Anthony Asquith and Leslie Howard
Producer: Gabriel Pascal
Stars: Leslie Howard as Higgins, Wendy Hiller as Liza, Scott Sunderland as Pickering, Wilfred Lawson as Doolittle, Marie Lohr as Mrs. Higgins

Major Barbara (1941)
Screenplay: Bernard Shaw

Director: Gabriel Pascal
Producer: Gabriel Pascal
Stars: Wendy Hiller as Barbara, Rex Harrison as Cusins, Robert Morley as Undershaft, Robert Newton as Bill Walker, Emlyn Williams as Snobby Price, Marie Lohr as Lady Britomart, Walter Hudd as Stephen

Caesar and Cleopatra (1945)
Screenplay: Bernard Shaw
Director: Gabriel Pascal
Producer: Gabriel Pascal (the Rank Organisation)
Stars: Claude Rains as Caesar, Vivien Leigh as Cleopatra, Flora Robson as Ftatateeta, Cecil Parker as Britannus, Basil Sidney as Rufio, Stewart Granger as Apollodorus

Appendix B

page 12

Beside Robert de Baudricourt's exclamation "Well I am damned!" is a question mark.

Two speeches below, "You will go to Paradise; and" is lined out.

page 13

Next to the line "Think of my boot; and take your backside out of reach of it" is a question mark.

page 19

Joan's "That is how the messages of God come to us" and Poulengey's comment "Checkmate" are lined out.

page 21

In Joan's speech beginning "We are all subject to the King of Heaven," the last line is amended to "You must not think about your duty to your feudal lord, but *more* about your duty to God" (my italics indicate the insert).

Robert de Baudricourt's "by Saint Denis!" "We are not talking about God," and "Damn you" are lined out.

page 23

A question mark is in the margin next to Joan's "Oh, squire! Your head is all circled with light like a saint's."

page 35

Beside the Archbishop's speech "(*Touched, putting his hand on her head*) Child: you are in love with religion" is written, "better to leave it [i.e., the line] out. Only the movement." An arrow extends from the comment to "But there is no danger" (two speeches below), which is underscored. "Reason for the cut" is written below the underscored line.

Joan's speech beginning "There is always danger" is lined out.

In the Archbishop's speech beginning "Gentlemen," the words "deadly sin" are underlined, and "another word instead" written beside them.

page 36

In Joan's second speech, "silly folks" is underlined.

page 41

In Joan's speech beginning "The land is thine," the words "become holy" are underlined. Next to the line is the substitute, "belong to god" [*sic*].

page 45

In Dunois's speech beginning "Is that all?" the word "infernal" is lined out.

pages 48–49

The dialogue beginning "I am like a man with two wives" (Dunois) through "never promised him" (Joan) is lined out.

page 51

Joan's stage direction, "kissing him on both cheeks," is lined out.

page 56

The sequence beginning "All stare horror-stricken" and ending "The Archer is already dead" is bracketed, with a large question mark beside it. In addition, parentheses enclose "Joan's cannon fires another shot."

page 65

In the speeches of the Chaplain and Cauchon, "His Eminence" is lined out. An explanation is in the margin: "This Title did not exist in those days. (Right Reverend)." [According to *The Oxford Dictionary of the Christian Church,* ed. F. L. Cross (London: Oxford University Press, 1957), p. 449, Pope Urban VIII in 1630 issued a decree confining the use of the title "His Eminence" to Cardinals. Prior to that date, they were called "Reverendissimi" (Most Reverend) or "Illustrissimi" (Most Illustrious).]

page 67

Joan's stage direction, "sits the crown on his head," is underlined. Beside it is written, " (The archbishop sits the crown on his head. Joan stands beside with the flag.) ."

The last three words in Cauchon's sentence, "The Church cannot take life," are underlined and above them written, "does not wish death."

In Joan's second speech, "Dear child of God" is lined out.

The sequence beginning with Joan's "I wish you were one of the village babies" and ending with the direction "lost in the distance" is lined out.

The dialogue from the Archbishop's "You forget yourself" through "as you are now speaking" (two speeches below) is crossed out.

In Dunois's speech, the statements "she thinks she has God in her pocket" and "And then she will find that God is on the side of the big battalions" are lined out.

Beneath "wolves fighting for pieces of her torn body" is a question mark, followed by "[illegible] be opened!"

Beside "The noise of battle" is written, "To develope?" [*sic*].

A line is drawn from Joan's "I have sworn as much as I will swear" through her "I should not have been here." Next to the first few speeches of this cut, the censor has written, "essentially damaging."

Joan's speech, "provided it does not demand anything impossible," is crossed out and "I appeal to god [*sic*] and to the pope [*sic*]" substituted. D'Estivet's reply is also crossed out and "The pope [*sic*] is far away from here. We can't reach him over there" substituted. [Although the censor's version is historically justified (proceedings of May 24, 1431), so is Shaw's (proceedings of March 31, 1431). Since several translations of the trial are available, I refer to the dates.]

pages 99–101

A line is drawn from Joan's "And in case the church should bid me do anything" through the Assessors' "Oh!"

page 102

To the right of Joan's "I will not" is written, " (Untill [*sic*] I shall be guarded by women instead of by men) " and to the left, " (historical reply) ." [The censor's paraphrase is accurate if misspelled. Shaw himself has a different paraphrase, in the fourth and sixth speeches below.]

page 104

The Inquisitor's speech beginning "The blessed Saint Athanasius" and Joan's reply are crossed out.

pages 104–5

Joan's speech beginning "Your torturer" and Ladvenu's statement, "That man is not only the torturer," are crossed out. Beside the passage is an illegible word.

page 106

Joan's "my voices promised me I should not be burnt" is lined out.

The sequence from Joan's "Oh, it is true" through Cauchon's "Amen!" is crossed out. Beside Joan's speech is written, "Its [*sic*] false and against the story and the truth."

page 107

The last six words of Cauchon's "You must sign a solemn recantation of your heresy" are lined out and "a declaration that you will not wear any longer [*sic*] masculine attire (mens cloths [*sic*]) and that you will submit to the churches [*sic*] decisions" written below.

page 108

Cauchon's "Read it to her" and Joan's "Do not trouble" are lined out. Next to the passage is the censor's explanation: "Declaration has not been read to Joan. As she could neither read nor write they did not trouble to tell her what she was to sign." [This assertion is related to the previous emendation, and derives from the view that Joan was told that she was signing an agreement not to wear men's clothes and to submit to the judgment of the Church, not that her voices were false. This interpretation is based not on the records of the trial but on the retrial of 1450, during which Jean Massieu testified that the abjuration which Joan signed was different from the abjuration reported in the records of the trial.]

pages 109–10

The dialogue from the Inquisitor's "You understand this, Joan?" through Joan's "ready for me in the market-place" is lined out.

page 111

In the second stage direction, the words "terrible anger" are lined out.

Following the third stage direction, Joan's question, "do you think I dread it as much as the life of a rat in a hole?" is lined out.

page 112

In Joan's speech, a line is drawn from "You think that life is nothing" through "from any human creature."

page 113

In Joan's speech beginning "His ways," the censor has lined out "for I am His child" through the end of the speech, and has written a substitute in the margin: "I appeal to god [*sic*] and the pope [*sic*]."

page 126

Before the speech beginning "Easy, Charlie, easy," the identification "Joan" is changed to "Joan's Voice." After the speech is the comment, " (Statue) in the room, then Joan herself [an illegible word] without movement like the statue."

TITLE

THE HUNDRED YEARS WAR
1429
FAIR FRANCE

"her cities and her towns defaced
By wasting ruin of the cruel foe." *

———————

Background of waste and ruin.

---

* Shaw misquotes Shakespeare's *King Henry VI,* part 1 (**III. iii.** 45–46) , substituting "her cities and her towns" for "the cities and the towns." Joan of Arc is a character in Shakespeare's play.

Appendix D BEGINNING OF SCENE ON THE LOIRE, EARLIER DRAFT

(NOTE: The scenes in the earlier draft, reproduced in Appendixes D through G, are numbered.)

SCENE 17.
The pennon streaming in the wind against the sky.

No other background.

DUNOIS looking up at it.

Only his head and shoulders.

DUNOIS, halting for a moment to glance up at the streaming pennon and shake his head wearily before he resumes his pacing, says:

DUNOIS
West wind, west wind, west wind. Strumpet: steadfast when you should be wanton, wanton when you should be steadfast. West wind on the silver Loire: what rhymes to Loire?

SCENE 18.
The pennon streaming, *close up,* against the sky as before.

DUNOIS' VOICE
Change, curse you, change. English harlot of a wind, change. West, west, I tell you.

SCENE 19.
The foreground of SCENE 16 ["Full landscape," i.e., long

shot], with the river bank, the
PAGE and DUNOIS pacing to
and fro *close up.*

DUNOIS
West wind, wanton wind, wilful
wind, womanish wind, false wind
from over the water, will you
never blow again?

A SENTRY'S VOICE WESTWARD
Halt! Who goes there?

Appendix E THE WIND CHANGES,
EARLIER DRAFT

SCENE 20.
Repeat SCENE 18.

The wind falls; and the pennon droops.

The wind rises from the opposite quarter.

The pennon streams violently in the new direction.

SCENE 21.
Repeat SCENE 17.

The PAGE looking up at the pennon.

Only his head is visible.

The PAGE, dropping the shield, calls excitedly after them:

PAGE
Seigneur! Seigneur! Mademoiselle!

Appendix F

D'ALENÇON

Yes; but you lent Him a hand, didnt you? Anyhow, the citizens think that it is you that have saved France. Theyre waiting for you at the city gate in thousands. You must ride in in triumph. Come along.

He seizes her by the wrist and drags her to the stairs.

JOAN, dragging back like a reluctant child, says:

JOAN

No, no: I want to pray; I want to be alone.

(*Weeping*)

Oh! Oh! Oh!

He drags her down ruthlessly.

SCENE 28.

In the palace of the Cardinal of Winchester. XIIIth Century architecture, in Rouen.

The CARDINAL, uncle to King Henry VI of England, is elderly and too fat. He is seated at breakfast, eating, and eating too much.

Serving men in waiting in sumptuous liveries.

152

DE STOGUMBER, a bullnecked English chaplain of 50, rushes in distractedly, with papers in his hand.

DE STOGUMBER
My lord, my lord, bad news, terrible news.

CARDINAL
Oh dear! Why do you bring me bad news at breakfast? I shall really have to get another secretary. You are so hot-headed! so thoughtless! so inconsiderate! And you know how easy it is to upset my digestion.

DE STOGUMBER
My lord, this is not a time to think of breakfast.

CARDINAL (*Yelling*)
What!!!

DE STOGUMBER
My lord, you m u s t give your mind to this. Orleans has fallen.

CARDINAL
Oh dear! dear! That comes of our commanders never being on speaking terms. No team work. Dear! dear! I told them so. *I* told them so.

DE STOGUMBER
My lord, you did not tell them that the sorceries of the abominable witch from Lorraine would

open the flaming pit of hell beneath their feet and swallow up Sir William Glasdale and all his men.

CARDINAL

Oh dear! dear! dear! I never liked Glasdale. But you may have some Masses said for him.

DE STOGUMBER

But that is not all, my lord. The witch is taking Charles to Rheims to crown him there.

CARDINAL

Well, why do they let her? There are plenty of troops to stop her. What is John Talbot doing?

DE STOGUMBER

My lord, Sir John Talbot is defeated and taken prisoner.

CARDINAL

Oh dear! He wont like that.

DE STOGUMBER

But do listen, my lord. There has been battle after battle, at Jargeau, at Meung, at Beaugency, at Patay. The witch has won them all. Our own troops, my lord, our Englishmen, who used to put the enemy to flight by the mere sound of their British cheers, are cowed and paralyzed at the sight of the witch's white banner. When they drive arrows through her throat the archers drop dead, and she rides on unharmed. Will not your lordship take the field and exorcise the devils that protect her and fight for her? It is not a task for sinful soldiers but for holy Churchmen.

CARDINAL

What! A cardinal stoop to exorcise a peasant girl! You forget my rank, Messire de Stogumber. Get some bishop to do it. Choose one of lowly birth. And now will you let me finish my breakfast before it is quite spoilt?

DE STOGUMBER

Is a breakfast spoilt a worse calamity than all France lost?

CARDINAL

France can wait half an hour. My breakfast cannot.

DE STOGUMBER

May I go to the Earl of Warwick about it?

CARDINAL

Yes, yes, yes. He's just the man to worry about such things. Off with you. Goodbye, goodbye.

DE STOGUMBER rushes out.

CARDINAL

Now my omelette is spoilt, I suppose.

BUTLER

Oh no, my lord. When you are delayed the cook begins a fresh one every half minute.

(*To the others*)

The omelette there!

The omelette is brought in and set before the CARDINAL.

CARDINAL

Ah! Good. Good. Good.

He falls to.

Appendix G BEGINNING OF THE SCENE IN THE MARKET PLACE, EARLIER DRAFT

SCENE 39.
Long shot.

Rouen. In the market place. Cheerful morning.

The preparation of the stake. Laborers, mostly women, hurrying in with great bundles of faggots on their backs.

A tall, almost monumental pile of sacks of sand, supports a platform of thick planks with a stake set up in it.

The EXECUTIONER has just fixed a chain round the stake, with an iron waist clasp attached to it. Kegs of oil are standing round him.

The EXECUTIONER's assistants are piling faggots and trusses of straw round the sacks, and throwing some of the trusses up to the platform.

Note: In this long shot the details will not be intelligible to the audience. The coup d'oeil will be of the whole market place, with the tall white pyre (the sacks will be white) in the centre.

SCENE 40.
Close up of the stake and platform. The top of a ladder projects into the bottom of the picture.

The EXECUTIONER catches the trusses of hay as they are thrown up from below, and arranges them round the stake.

Then he takes a mallet; knocks in the heads of the keys; and pours the oil over the trusses.

He is cheerful, busy, and whistles or hums a tune occasionally, like a man whose business is flourishing.

Whistling or humming heard occasionally.

If a bird or two could be induced to light on the stake, the effect would be more deadly.

Finally, the EXECUTIONER looks round to see that all is complete, and rubs his hands with satisfaction.

He goes down the ladder.

Appendix H AN ALTERNATE ENDING

Dissolves

to an equestrian statue of THE
MAID (Place de Rivoli, Paris)
—cutting in from the lower
edge. It is silhouetted against
the rays of the sun and the
gilt armor glistens.

The noise of the modern city
is heard, the throbbing of
motor car engines, horns, the
cries of newspaper boys, etc.

Fade out.

THE END.

Appendix I ANOTHER ALTERNATE ENDING

The sound of church bells is heard first as if coming from afar, but then approaching nearer and nearer. More and more bells. On the dark screen there appears the date "May 16th 1920" on a parchment document.

The camera slowly moves away, bringing into view the whole of the document, which contains the Canonization of Joan of Arc by the Vatican. Finally in semi-profile a high dignitary of the Church is seen putting his signature under this document. He is an old man and the view is obliquely from the back (Pope Benedict XVth).

The camera now moves further away and reveals—

A HALL IN THE VATICAN.

The POPE sits enthroned and is surrounded by his CARDINALS. The picture gradually

dissolves

(The peals of the Church bells increasing in volume during the whole of the time) *into*

THE DOME OF ST PETER'S.

The camera pans down, again moving away until the grandiose view into the Piazzo St Pietro fills the screen.

Dissolve to

The sides of the square are lined with gazing people anxious to catch a glimpse of this unique and rare spectacle.

Dissolve to

THE INTERIOR OF ST PETER'S.

Slowly comes into view the magnificent and colorful spectacle of the procession of the CARDINALS entering St Peter's from the Vatican.

Together with the CARDINALS appears the entire Holy Court. The dignitaries assemble—and the picture culminates in the entry of the POPE himself surrounded by Church dignitaries.

The POPE is in full ornate wearing the tiara on his head. He takes his seat in their midst.

Superimposed over this ceremonious spectacle there appears the visionary head of St

Joan, gradually becoming clearer and larger.

Music, the organ, and the "White Choir."

The volume of sound slowly increases and the picture gradually

fades out.

(*Note:* The pictures of the Canonization of St Joan in Rome naturally excel by the magnificence and beauty of their color. They seem to call for a reproduction in color and the Producer therefore contemplates the possibility of using the color film for these scenes.)